MAP TO HAPPINESS

MAP TO HAPPINESS

Straightforward Advice on Everyday Issues

The Reverend Peter K. Stimpson

iUniverse, Inc.
New York Lincoln Shanghai

MAP TO HAPPINESS
Straightforward Advice on Everyday Issues

iUniverse books may be ordered through booksellers or by contacting:

iUniverse
2021 Pine Lake Road, Suite 100
Lincoln, NE 68512
www.iuniverse.com
1-800-Authors (1-800-288-4677)

Because of the dynamic nature of the Internet, any Web addresses or links contained in this book may have changed since publication and may no longer be valid.

The views expressed in this work are solely those of the author and do not necessarily reflect the views of the publisher, and the publisher hereby disclaims any responsibility for them.

ISBN: 978-0-595-48057-9 (pbk)
ISBN: 978-0-595-71659-3 (cloth)
ISBN: 978-0-595-60155-4 (ebk)

Printed in the United States of America

ACKNOWLEDGMENT

This book would not have been possible
without the support of
my good friend,
Martin Chooljian.

CONTENTS

CHAPTER TWO

COMMON PATHS TO HAPPINESS

CHAPTER THREE

CHAPTER FOUR

PREFACE
WHO AM I?

"Oh no, not another book on happiness! What's so special about this one? Is it worth buying? Or is it just more optimistic dribble to make me feel better and to make the author rich? Who is this guy anyway? What makes him the big expert on what will make me happy?"

When you saw this book, was that what went through your mind? Well, those are fair questions to ask. So, let me briefly tell you who I am and why I wrote this book.

My name is Peter Stimpson. I am a priest and a therapist. I was ordained a priest in 1972, and while my desire was to serve as a parish priest, I was asked to teach religion at The Vincentian Institute, a high school in Albany, New York, which I did until 1975.

During those three years, I not only had a number of students coming to me for counseling, but also many adults at the parish where I was living. While I had a degree in pastoral theology, I still recognized my need to deepen my knowledge of counseling, and so I decided to enter the School of Social Work at the State University of New York at Albany.

Upon graduation, I became the Executive Director of the Counseling Service of the Episcopal Diocese of Albany, serving there from 1977-1989, until taking the position of Executive Director of Trinity Counseling Service in Princeton, New Jersey in 1989, where I remain today. Over the last thirty years, I have counseled people from all walks of life: corporate executives and construction workers, atheists and priests, rich and poor, and all have found my combination of psychology and theology to have provided them with an insight and link that had been missing.

During this time, I was encouraged to write an advice column, beginning in 1983 when I entitled it, "Hints for Happiness" in a newspaper of the Diocese of

Albany called *Via Media*. My desire was to pass along my insights so as to make the journey of the reader happier and less troublesome. The articles were so well received that when I moved to Princeton, New Jersey, I was asked to write my column for the newspaper of the Diocese of New Jersey, and then even for a Princeton newspaper called *Town Topics*.

Over the years, my readers have continually asked that I convert these articles into a book, so as to share my insights with as many people as possible. This is what I have now done. My sole desire is to help you. Please realize that my voice is but one among many. While I think that I have many valuable insights to impart, and a perspective missing in many other such books, I realize that I am one voice among many. I come to you, therefore, not as a guru sitting atop a mountain arrogantly handing out pearls of wisdom, but as a person who has spent my life in the trenches with you, and who humbly offers you some of what I have learned along the way.

So, I would urge you to momentarily put whatever cynicism you may have on the back burner, and give this book a chance. If I am wrong, use the book to kindle your next fire. If I am right, you will feel better and want to give the book to someone you love. So, take a chance and turn the page.

INTRODUCTION

You are busy. Stress is your daily companion. You yearn for help, but your hectic schedule, whether raising children or commuting to work, cries out for advice that gets to the point.

Life can be confusing, many becoming lost while pursuing happiness. You would like help, but not if it is going to give you more stress to get it. You would prefer simple answers to complex problems. Not simple in being simplistic, but rather in sifting through confusing issues to their core, and then offering easy-to-understand explanations that convert into ready-to-use solutions.

While I am sure that sounds good to you, my desire is not to just be one more self-help book spitting out sage answers to perplexing problems, but also and primarily to arm you with key principles with which to not only answer a specific problem that you are facing today, but also to answer any problem that you may face in all your tomorrows. These principles offer a unique perspective, enabling you to look at old issues in new ways. That perspective is the primary gift of the book for you.

In writing this book, my intent has been neither to cover every issue, nor to cover any issue from every conceivable angle, but rather to give you a map to guide you through whatever issues life presents to an ever-increasing sense of happiness. What I offer is just the opinion of one man, who, while having the expertise and experience of both a priest and a therapist, is still himself continuing on the same journey as you are. I do not have all the answers, and remain open to learn from others, just as I hope you can learn from me. And, as I am a priest, there is no question that I approach issues from a Judeo-Christian perspective. While this will speak to many in our culture, it certainly does not imply that it is the only perspective, just that it is mine.

The format of the book is to address each issue by first showing you actual questions that I have received for an advice column that I have been writing since 1983. I include these questions to show you that my answers are not simply drawn from my personal reflections, but also from addressing the pain of others. My guess is that these questions are applicable to many people, and so might hopefully address some of your pain.

Finally, as you begin to find happiness, realize that this is only the tip of the iceberg. Allow me to show you how to continually increase your happiness, never reaching a plateau where you merely coast, but always finding a new world where you can explore and grow, no matter what life throws at you.

CHAPTER ONE
A MAP TO GUIDE YOU

If you take a trip, you first need to know where you are going. If you would like to journey towards happiness, then we need to address some rather basic questions. What is the meaning of your life? Why were you born? And, what exactly is happiness?

Hidden within the answers to these questions are principles to guide your journey. Once you are armed with these principles, then you will be able to apply those insights into every aspect of your life, allowing you to see answers that might have previously been hidden from you.

A. What is the Purpose of Your Life?

QUESTION: Recently I woke up in the middle of the night in a cold sweat, sat up straight, and realized that I'm getting older and will one day die. I can't seem to stop worrying, the question that haunts me being: What is the meaning of my life? Does my life have a purpose?

QUESTION: I just celebrated my 65th birthday. I have worked hard all my life, and yet when I look back, I wonder what it was all for. Why was I born? Why was anyone born?

QUESTION: What is happiness? When I was a kid, it was to win ballgames. When I became an adult, it was to make money. But, I've never really gotten there. My wife tells me that I'm never happy and that my moods turn people off, but time is running out.

ANSWER

We all wonder what the purpose of our life is. The issue is so big that it scares us, causing us to avoid facing it, the result being that one day this repressed issue comes frighteningly bubbling to the surface. As the answer is essential to determine how we shall pursue happiness, let us look at it honestly instead of ducking it. So, why were you born?

TO LIVE FOREVER? **No.** You can eat health foods until they come out of your ears, exercise to the point of making Arnold Schwarzenegger jealous, drink the standard 8 glasses of water a day, have more cosmetic surgery than Cher and Demi Moore combined, and 100 years from now, you will be dead.

TO BECOME RICH? **No.** Oh, don't get me wrong. Material wealth is nice to have, but you must share it, and you cannot take it with you. I have often joked with people that their Lexus will not fit into their coffin with them, but their soul will, it being ironic how much time we spend on things that do not last. Think of all the riches that were buried with the Pharaohs to help them on the journey to the next life, only to have people in this life steal them.

TO BECOME FAMOUS? **No.** Read *People* magazine. Fame is fleeting. The adoration of the masses can leave as quickly as it comes, and can be falsely placed, based on performance instead of personality, and occasionally based on behavior that is more ignominious than renown.

TO HAVE POWER? **No.** Again, that does not endure. Think of Alexander the Great, Caesar and Napoleon. They conquered, or tried to conquer, the world. But today, they are but a memory. Reflect upon Percy Bysshe Shelley's 1817 poem, "Ozymandias", where he contemplates on a decaying statue of Ramses II, contrasting the arrogant words of the ancient Pharaoh *("My name is Ozymandias, king of kings. Look on my works, ye Mighty and despair!")* with the sorry state and empty surroundings of his statue *("Nothing else remains, Round the decay of that colossal wreck").*

TO LOVE AND BE LOVED? **Yes.** You are defined by the choices you make. Each interaction with each person on each day of your life is an opportunity for you to grow or shrink, to love or hate. You can be kind or cruel, helpful or manipulative, cooperative or controlling.

HAPPINESS

What then is happiness? It is **a process, not a product**. It is not something you buy, but a process of becoming. You do not have to be a corporate executive, make a six-figure income, and drive a BMW to be happy. These things are certainly nice, but my point is that **what** you attain is less important than **how** you attain it. It is how we relate to others that determines our degree of happiness.

Think about it. You are loved by your spouse and children not for all the hours you worked or goodies you provided, but rather for those qualities that made spending time with you a joy, such as your sensitivity, caring, reliability and responsibility.

Those qualities are internal. They are part of you, defining who you are, your very soul. Both this life and the next will be enriched or impoverished by the depth of those qualities, rewarding you with the closeness of friends or punishing you with the loneliness of a selfish heart. The judgment of God will be to simply accept your own free-will judgment, made over a lifetime to be experienced for eternity.

Therefore, you were born to become fully human, fully mature, and fully happy. Who you are inside will go with you from this life to the next. What you have on the outside, whether possessions or acclaim, will not. Do not despair for not having enough of the latter, but for your sake, seize every day you have left to add to the former, to add to who you are meant to become, a work of art.

A PICTURE OF HEAVEN AND HELL

Still a bit confused? Well, let us look at this from another angle. My belief is that the purpose of life is to make a simple choice between good or evil, our answer being shown less by what we say and more by what we do, our actions speaking louder than our words. For those who are religious, those choices on earth affect how we shall live after death.

If you choose to view others as suckers of whom you can take advantage instead of as potential friends, then you fail to learn how to be close to them, condemning yourself to be lonely, frustrated, and angry. When you are placed in the presence of God after death, never having learned how to be close to others, you do not know how to be close to God, nor to all who have died before you: your mom and dad, brothers and sisters, uncles and aunts, and all your friends. Then you look around and see many who are close, and, therefore, happy. All of a sudden, you realize that this state of emptiness will last for all eternity. *You are in Hell.*

However, if, during your lifetime, you give of yourself and thus receive love and friendship in return, you may not be rich or famous, but you will possess the secret of life, that is, knowing how to love. When placed in the presence of God and of all your family and friends, you will be able to be close to them, your reward being eternal happiness. *You are in Heaven.*

Still too complicated? Then on the premise that a picture is worth a thousand words, here is the answer that I gave to a little boy who once asked me what heaven and hell were like. It worked so well that now I use it with adults.

I told him to imagine entering into a big house in which there were only two rooms, one marked "Heaven" and one marked "Hell".

First, you look into the room marked "Hell". You see a large banquet table with all your favorite foods: turkey with all the fixings, roast beef, ham, corn, peas, ice cream, cakes, pies, and everything your heart desires. There are no liver, lima beans or brussels sprouts. But all the knives, forks and spoons are eight feet long, and you cannot eat without using the utensils. So, Hell is being so close and yet so far from all that luscious food.

Then you peek into the room marked "Heaven". It is the same picture! All your favorite foods are set before you, and you must use the eight-foot utensils to eat. But, because you were caring instead of selfish during your lifetime, it occurs to you that you can reach out and feed the person sitting across from you.

Hence, those in Heaven are having a party, where those in Hell are starving to death, worrying how they are going to get that food into their mouths without the other people stealing it from them.

The situation is the same, but the two groups see it differently, having learned to love or not love during their lives on earth. One can easily see the solution; the other is blind.

CONCLUSION

God gives us free will. The judgment of God is to accept your judgment. The punishment for choosing to be selfish is to **be** selfish. It saddens God if you choose to not love Him or your fellow human beings, but that is your choice. You choose to be happy or sad, to be in heaven or hell. He provides eternal life. You determine how you will live it.

You should not wait to make this choice on your deathbed, but do so every day of your life. If you are on the wrong path, then wake up and change! If you are on the right path, then do not become smug and complacent, just keep going. Go to church or synagogue to continue to learn more about the purpose of life and be refreshed for the challenges of each day. Then love your family, give an honest day's labor at work, treat all people as you would want to be treated, and worry not about the end of this life. The next one will be very happy.

B. Three Principles

QUESTION: I have been reading your column for a few years, and finally decided to write and ask you a tough question. Are there any secrets about life that you have learned in counseling others that many never seem to learn? If so, what are they?

ANSWER

The question of this person sparked a great deal of thought. I said to myself, if the purpose of life is to choose who we are by how we relate to others, and if happiness is that lifetime process of becoming more by loving more, then why cannot more people follow those simple ideas to a better life? If life is about making choices, then how can people be guided to make the right choices?

What I have discovered is that there are three principles that are necessary keys to unlock the door to your happiness. Without them, people take the wrong turn on the road. They are simple concepts, but they so elude people that I once called them "secrets". As they are crucial in your quest to find happiness, let us now expose those secrets.

1. **INSECURITY:** *The first principle is that all people feel insecure.* This may come as a shock to you; it sure was to me. Growing up, I had this image that on the other side of the hill were all these "normal" people, and that when I went through that magic door into adulthood at age 21, I would be like them.

Well, I am now 61 and there is no magic door. I have counseled people from all walks of life to whom others often turn for advice, such as clergy, doctors, lawyers, professors, college presidents, corporate executives, as well as others who are rich and famous, and they all have one thing in common, they are human! They are just as insecure as you and me. If they honestly admit and face their clay feet, they grow. If they hide behind masks of superiority, making you think that they "have it all together", they don't.

So, stop chasing a ghost. There are no perfect people. We all feel insecure. If the pursuit of happiness is a process, does it really make sense that on one sunny day you will attain total security and perfection? Of course not. Accepting our limits does not mean settling, just being more patient and forgiving each time we trip and fall. It also means taking a blindfold off to see those who arrogantly look down upon us not as heroes to emulate, but rather as pathetic souls who are lost and unwilling to face life as it is instead of how they portray it.

2. **POWER:** *The second principle is to take back the power to define our own worth.*

Once you realize that everyone is insecure, it no longer makes sense to look to others to tell you whether you are good or bad. Of course, growing up you must rely upon your parents to help you begin to understand your self worth. For example, by taking the time to not only put your kindergarten artwork on the refrigerator, but also to admire and inquire about it, you begin to see your worth mirrored back to you in their eyes.

But if your parents do not help you to think for yourself, or measure your worth upon performance, you will probably continue to give the power to define your worth to other significant people who cross your path, such as your teachers, employers, and spouse. You will always want to avoid criticism and get praise, nervously awaiting your grades at school or your evaluation at work, for if they are bad, then tragically you think that you are bad.

Thus, giving away your power condemns you to always worry about what others think. The secret is to take back your power, and define your own self-worth. Once you rely upon your own judgment about yourself, it is as if you are wearing a psychological suit of armor. Others can hurt your feelings, but their demeaning criticism can no longer devastate you to the core. Why? Because *you*, not they, have the power.

3. **SUCCESS:** *The third principle is that success is more about **who** you become and less about **what** you attain.*

Once you take back the power to define your worth, then it is as if blind-ers are removed from the eyes of your soul. Not worrying about impressing others, you can finally concentrate on what matters most, that is, *who* you are becoming.

Most people want to show others how successful they have become. As they have given the power to define their worth outside of themselves, they look for outside symbols by which to impress others. They equate success as attaining something big, such as a job, house, car, bank account, et cetera. If they do not, they feel small; they feel like a failure. But, while there is really nothing wrong with pursuing achievements, where these people get mixed up is in not real-izing that achievements are the "little goal".

The "big goal" is how your personality develops along the way to attaining the little goal. Homer once said, "The journey is the thing". Your job will end with a gold watch, your house will pass to someone else, your car will rust at the town dump, but your soul will live forever. As I have said, who you become is defined by the choices you make in life: to be kind or cruel, loving or manipulative, humble or a snob. So, why not pay attention to what lasts, instead of racing after what eventually disappears.

Life is a process of creating a work of art, YOU. Your death signals the end of your growth, and the judgment of God is to simply accept your judgment, allowing you to be for eternity the person whom you have chosen to become as defined by your actions on earth.

So, don't get mixed up; the big goal is **who** you become—the little goal is **what** you attain. Make sure that you do not put the proverbial cart in front of the horse.

In conclusion, what are the **Three Principles**, the keys that will unlock your mind to see what path to travel?

1. **INSECURITY**: Do not worry about feeling insecure. We all do. So, be forgiving of yourself and patient in your growth process.

2. **POWER**: If everyone is insecure, then stop giving others the power to determine your worth.

3. **SUCCESS**: And, if you no longer need to impress others to feel good about yourself, realizing that happiness is a process of *personal* growth, then reach for what will last, focusing more on **who** you become (big goal) than **what** you attain (little goal).

SUMMARY
Your Pocket Map

<u>**PURPOSE OF LIFE**</u>: To choose **who** you are by **how** you relate to others.

<u>**HAPPINESS**</u>: Not a onetime product you buy, but a lifetime process of *becoming*, growing through choices that deepen your love of self and others.

<u>**TO MAKE THE RIGHT CHOICES**</u>: Follow three principles:

1. <u>**INSECURITY**</u>: Do not worry about feeling insecure. We all do. So, be forgiving of yourself and patient in your growth process.

2. <u>**POWER**</u>: If everyone is insecure, then stop giving them the power to determine your worth.

3. <u>**SUCCESS**</u>: And, if you no longer need to impress others to feel good about yourself, realizing that happiness is a process of personal growth, then reach for what will last, focusing more on **who** you become (*big goal*) than **what** you attain (*little goal*).

THE PROCESS OF *BECOMING* HAPPIER

INSECURITY---------------→ POWER---------------→SUCCESS
If we are all insecure---→then take back the power---→and reach for what
to define your worth   will last.

H A P P I N E S S

CHAPTER TWO

COMMON PATHS TO HAPPINESS

There are many paths to happiness. What follows is not an attempt to explain the only ways, but rather just to shed light on some of the more common ways.

A. Loving Yourself

I often will ask people in counseling what their priorities are, that is, in what order of importance they would place themselves, their spouse and their children. Invariably, people say, "Well, my kids would definitely come first, then my spouse, and then me."

I would then try to help them understand that they had their priorities upside down. If you do not love yourself enough, then you will not be strong and self-confident enough to effectively love your spouse, to stimulate their personal growth and their intimacy with you. And unless you have a healthy marriage, you will be weakened in being able to emotionally feed your children.

This is a hard concept for us to master, as we have often been trained to think that a primary focus upon ourselves is selfish. Nothing could be further from the truth. But, decide for yourself as you read the next few sections that are ordered with *you* coming first.

1. Is Self-Care Selfish?

QUESTION: Why does religion always make you feel guilty when you do something for yourself? I'm not a selfish person, but I usually feel bad when I do something good for myself. Why?

ANSWER

Self-Care is **not** *Selfish*. Taking care of yourself does not automatically imply not caring for others.

While many well-meaning religion teachers drummed into us the need to "give till it hurts", both Jewish and Christian scriptures tell us to "love your neighbor *as you love yourself*" (Leviticus 19:18 & Matthew 22:39, Mark 12:30 and Luke 10:27). We tend to forget about the second half of that advice. Think about it, if you do not love yourself well, then you will not be empowered to love your neighbor well. Let me give you a few examples, some with references to the bible, to help you understand what I mean.

1. **ASSERTIVENESS**: If you never learn to say "No", your ubiquitous "Yes" will lead you towards "burn out" and resentment of others.

    Suppose someone asks you to help them move but you have a bad back, or your pastor asks you to run the annual bazaar but you have a demanding job and a neglected spouse. Not saying "no" leads to muscle spasms, terse words that make everyone cringe and wish they never asked for your help, and more than a few arguments with your spouse. Even if all goes miraculously well, people tend to then ask you for more! So, setting realistic limits leads to more respect from others and less stress for you.

2. **DELEGATING**: Moses learned to delegate to Judges (Exodus 18:13-26) and 70 Elders (Numbers 11:16-17), and Jesus to 12 Apostles (Mark 3:13-19). Climbing any corporate ladder usually depends upon letting go of the perfectionistic thought that "if you want it done right, you have to do it yourself."

3. **MEDITATING**: While the Apostles were always guiltily urging Jesus to move to the next town where many were waiting to be healed, he instead would often go to the desert to pray, to re-create, re-center, and refresh himself (Matthew 14:22, Mark 3:7 and Luke 5:15). If we took just 5 min-

utes a day to do the same, the stresses and strains of daily life would shrink in importance, as would our headaches and ulcers.

4. **CARE OF YOUR BODY**: If Moses or Jesus were physically and emotionally exhausted, cynical, disillusioned, overweight, depressed and chain smokers, who would have seriously listened to them? There is nothing wrong with taking time for daily exercise, healthy meals, and a good night's rest. Working 12-hour days speckled with fast foods and few breaks leads to being overly tired, far less creative, ironically less productive, and possibly dying too young. How is that supposed to help others?

In conclusion, to your surprise, religion actually encourages you to take good care of yourself. For it takes a healthy you to effectively care for others.

2. The Need to be Noticed

QUESTION: Everyone tries to be a big deal, to brag about what they have done right and deny what they did wrong. They always strut their stuff in front of others to the point that they make me sick to my stomach. Why do so many act that way?

ANSWER

What is behind the need of a person to be noticed? Well, remember the principle about power? Who holds the power to determine your worth? You or someone else?

Overcritical parents unwittingly convey that love is conditional upon performance. Unless you get an "A", hit a home run, get into the right college, and marry the right person, your worry is that criticism and rejection will greet you with chagrin at the front door. Not surprisingly, as you grow older, you subconsciously transfer that power to bring you up or down to others, like your teacher, your boss, or your spouse. Getting fired or divorced become fates worse than death, loudly proclaiming to all what a "loser" you are.

If you have given others the power to determine your worth, then you try to please them, turning yourself into a psychological pretzel to be noticed. You try to tip the scales by bragging about your accomplishments and denying your failures. Even if all goes well, you are always waiting for the other shoe to drop, for someone to peal back the mask of your phony facade and see the "real you". Hence, being on top today means nothing tomorrow, and you have to daily drag yourself out of bed to wearily climb that mountain again and again, endlessly hungering for others to give you a nod.

A few years ago, I traveled to Italy, and what struck me was how this same theme repeats throughout time. The biggest statues in St. Peter's in Rome are of the Popes, the palaces of the Medici in Florence have their pictures and statutes splashed throughout most rooms, and the paintings of Jesus or Mary in the Palace of the Doge in Venice usually have the Doge strategically in the picture as if he already had one foot in heaven.

So, if you are bothered by those who arrogantly claim to be "on the inner track" and not-so-subtly shove their bigger car and house in your face, realize that they are lost in an upside-down world where their value is out of their control, feeling condemned to anxiously compete in order to survive. Instead of jealously joining their epistemological worldview, why not realize that your worth is internal, not external, that is, determined by who you are, not what others think.

Loving yourself, therefore, means seeing life through the lens of our principles of both power and success. As regards the latter, remember that what lasts is not the position you hold or the power you wield, but rather the person whom you choose to become. Titles and positions are at best recorded in a dusty book that few read, whereas your soul vibrantly travels en toto from this life to the next. Your integrity and intuition, responsibility and reliability, sensitivity and caring, and your ability to give and receive love are the true testaments to who you have chosen to become, and most importantly are defined by you, not others. These are not tarnished by a bad economy, a bad marriage, ill health or even an early death. However, they can be damaged by you, if you choose to compromise who you are due to being fooled into playing the game of the insecure bragger, endlessly chasing the ghost of happiness that is always just out of your grasp.

OUR MAP: *Loving Yourself*

PRINCIPLES and PROBLEMS
How our principles helped solve these problems.

POWER: You are of great worth. Therefore, you need neither feel guilty for caring for yourself, nor dance to the tune of others to be noticed.

SUCCESS: Your enduring personality is more important than the passing position you hold or the power you wield.

FURTHER READING

- Brander, Nathaniel, The Six Pillars of Self-Esteem, New York, Bantam, 1994.
- Burns, David, Ten Days to Self-Esteem, New York, Harper Collins Publishers, 1993.
- Domar, Alice D., and Henry Dreher, Self-Nurture: Learning to Care for Yourself As Effectively As You Care for Everyone Else, New York, Penguin Books, 2000.
- Sanford, Linda Tschirhart, and Mary Ellen Donovan, Women & Self-Esteem, New York, Penguin Books, 1984.
- Wilde, Stuart, Infinite Self, London, Hay House, 1996.

B. Loving Your Spouse

1. Falling in Love

QUESTION: Can someone really "fall in love"? Each time the chemistry has been there with what seems like a great guy, I've gotten burned. I don't get it. Why?

ANSWER

Can you really "fall in love"? When someone "falls head over heels" in love, it seems to imply a magical and secret component to their relationship. Yet, the presence of love should not imply the absence of thought.

Many a priest in pre-marital counseling groans when the couple draws a blank at the question, "What do you love about one another?" Serious doubt is indicated if, after much reflection, the answers indicate little depth, such as "because she's a real fox", "he's fun to be with", or, once to my horror, "because we like the same kind of pizza". While the couple may look upon the priest as if he or she has callously cast doubt on the love story of the century, nonetheless, a little work now could save a lot of heartache later.

So, after serious thought, many couples are able to trace their attraction to such fine qualities as empathy, selflessness, and a willingness to communicate in an open and honest manner with one another. They are also able to spot areas of needed growth, and to develop a plan that will get their marriage off on the right foot.

But, some people are often "burned" not only because they let their heart rule their head, but also because they look for marriage to heal old wounds from parents or former spouses. We are often attracted to people who are psychologically carbon copies of that parent by whom we never felt accepted. Unconsciously, we hope that if we can make our spouse love us, then maybe we could have gotten our parents to love us. As we have made our one spouse equal two persons, we are willing to endure a fair amount of abuse before we give up trying to win over that person.

If a divorce occurs, amazingly many people fall in love again with a similar type of person. I can remember once having a husband come into therapy with his sixth wife, telling both her and me how unlucky he was to have "gotten stuck with six losers in a row". That endearing comment earned him another divorce, but therapy thankfully helped him see his continual attraction to the same kind of person, his need to mourn instead of repeat the past, and to come finally to love and accept himself.

Therefore, the point is that no one really falls in love. Those who describe "love at first sight", followed by a quick marriage, are lucky if it works. With the divorce rate being what it is, consider taking luck out of the process. Look before you leap. Discover what you love about a person, as well as how you can help each other grow. While this may sometimes be hard, it will always be healthy.

<u>KEY POINTS</u>

- You do not *fall* in love.
- Love is the heart's reaction to the mind's perception.
- Your mind sees not only how you look on the outside, but also who you are on the inside: sensitive, caring, thoughtful, responsible, reliable, etc.
- Too little thought at the beginning leads to too much pain later.

2. What Does "I Love You" Mean?

QUESTION: Married couples say "I love you" so freely, or perhaps I should say "loosely". I don't think many people know what those words really mean. As a priest and a marriage counselor, what would be your explanation?

ANSWER

Well, if one does not really fall in love, then what really attracts us to someone? What does it mean when someone says, "I love you"? Here are eight points to consider.

1. **MIND & HEART**: Love is an attraction to what is perceived as good. Your mind has to see the worth of a person before your heart can express your affection. Love, therefore, is not a whimsical emotion, but rather a reaction to the depth and majesty of the other. If I asked you if you liked a movie before you even saw it, you would tell me that is impossible. Precisely, that is my point.

2. **THE EYES OF THE OTHER**: To drive my point home, when a person feels insecure, I often ask them why their spouse loves them. Could it be your spouse is just stupid and cannot see what a loser you are? Or, could they see what a nice person is hiding underneath that rough exterior? My facetious comment makes a person see their own value reflected back to them in the eyes of their lover.

3. **A COVENANT**: Love in marriage is not a boring, stagnant, legal contract carved in stone that locks you into a relationship, but rather a living breathing commitment to ongoing growth with one another. Your vow keeps interference out and intensity in, essentially serving as a protective bubble. Burst the bubble by weakening the relationship, letting any third party water down the intensity of your relationship, and that empty feeling is the price you pay.

4. **BRAVE**: Love means having the courage to ask the other person to grow. Perhaps that means learning to argue with sensitivity instead of aggression, or to be humble yourself instead of wearing a mask of superiority.

5. **PATIENT**: If a person is genuinely trying to grow, the speed of that growth is less important. They may be weak where you are strong, and so have to grow according to their time clock, not yours. Remember, your spouse will have to be patient with you too!

6. **KIND**: Growth requires sandpaper and blankets. Sandpaper for the growing edge, but blankets for kindness. If you come across as arrogant and demanding, trying to control and manipulate, all you will get is defensiveness, procrastination, and broken promises. Your spouse does not want a teacher, just a lover.

7. **FORGIVING**: In this journey prompted by love, all of us make mistakes, say insensitive, sarcastic, and cruel things to win arguments or in retaliation for feeling hurt. What should you do? Punish the other, extracting your pound of flesh? No. The punishment for being selfish is to **be** selfish. Instead, if the person is truly sorry, give them another chance as forgiveness is based less on the person forgiving being nice, and more on the person being forgiven having the potential for change.

8. **DON'T BE ENVIOUS**: If your spouse showers your children, family and friends with love, that is not taking anything away from you. Love is not a quantity, so that you are getting less of the pie. It is a quality. The more your spouse exercises his or her love for others, the better able they become to love you.

3. Finding the Right Person

QUESTION: A lot of relationships blossom due to the romantic appeal of Valentine's Day. Is that enough to keep a relationship going? I suppose it isn't, but how do you find the right person?

ANSWER

Even knowing what love is, you may still have a hard time finding the "right" person. It is amazing to me that living in a sophisticated society, one where everyone realizes that hard work in college and on the job is essential for success, that we still cling to the notion that there is a perfect person out there somewhere, and that the fortunes of fate will somehow magically enable you to bump into one another. And, if you luck out and meet a nice person, often people think, "What can go wrong if the chemistry is right?" The answer: Plenty!

Hence, why not take luck out of the process, and begin to decide what is best for *you*, then using your dates to see if Prince Charming or Cinderella actually "measure up". What does that mean? Here are a few suggestions.

1. **ARE THEY AVAILABLE?** If you are drawn to someone who is either married or separated, trouble abounds. Oh sure, they tell you tales of woe about their miserable, soon-to-be ex-spouse, but all too often, your feelings will be crushed beneath the surprising news that they are going to try to "work it out" with their spouse. So, unless they are free, flee.

2. **ARE THEY MATURE?** If you feel like they are selling a product, don't buy. Look for someone who is reasonably confident in their self-worth, as evidenced by them admitting their flaws, instead of endlessly telling you about how big their job, house, car, or bank account is. If they are talking about how they are going to take care of "poor little you", that is a sign that they are attracted to you because of your perceived weakness. Once you grow up, you will grow out of them.

3. **WHY ARE YOU IN LOVE?** What qualities of the person attract you? When people are unsure, but respond that "the chemistry is right", I get the wrong feeling. As I said a little while ago, if someone felt unloved by a parent, they subconsciously are often attracted to someone who has a similar personality, the hidden hope being that if they can get this person to love them in

the present, maybe they could have gotten their parent to love them in the past. This often explains why someone puts up with abusive behavior, long after family and friends have advised them to "dump" this person.

4. **WILL THEY WAIT?** Often, men and women feel pressured to have sex, if not on the 1st date, certainly by the 3rd or 4th date, their fear being that the other person will leave them unless they "put out". Why "sell out" for love? If someone truly is mature and truly loves you, they will wait, realizing that to physically "make love" to someone before you are psychologically "in love" is irrational.

5. **DO YOU LOVE YOURSELF?** To plunge into a relationship too early and too deep is a sign that you may be too insecure, feeling that if you do not act now, all will be lost. Yet, true love is based on your true value, namely, such qualities as your kindness, sensitivity, intelligence, responsibility, and commitment. Act in haste because you feel desperate, and you will have to repent in leisure with a painful divorce. So, go slow for a relationship that will last. The point is, you deserve it!

4. Feeding Your Marriage

QUESTION: My husband and I have been married for 6 years. We met and fell in love during a flight to Florida. It was magical. We were instantly drawn to each other. It just felt right. Now we seem to be drifting apart. If it was so right at the beginning, how could it ever go wrong?

ANSWER

Once you are happily married, you want to stay that way. If you do not feed your marriage, it will starve to death. The beginning of your relationship was a bit like the wondrous month of April. Flowers are blooming, birds are singing, and love is in the air. But, for love to last, for it to endure beyond April, our heads must guide our hearts. A lasting marriage depends upon the attraction lasting long after the removal of the rose-colored glasses. So, here are just a few hints of how to continually breathe life into your marriage.

1. **TALK**: Couples should talk a minimum of 1 hour per week. While this is easy while dating, it becomes more difficult when you have 3 children continually interrupting you. Nonetheless, you should not put communication on the back burner, for when the last child leaves the nest, you do not want to gaze across the kitchen table at a stranger. So, get creative. Plop a disk in the DVD player for the kids to enjoy, or hire a babysitter and go out, but whatever you do, make room to listen and adjust to the changing goals and dreams of your spouse.

2. **ARGUE**: Did I say argue? Yes. Unless you marry your clone, you are going to have differences that need to be resolved. So, some of your talks may be arguments, where each of you is brave enough to bare your soul, telling the other how you have been hurt, and how you can work together to be more caring. Arguing does not mean yelling or being sarcastic. It means being assertive plus sensitive, assertive to openly reveal what is on your mind, and sensitive to cushion your words so as to lead to empathy instead of defensiveness.

3. **FORGIVE**: We all make mistakes. If after arguing, your spouse apologizes, and then backs that up with changed behavior, do not hold a grudge or seek revenge, but instead realize that forgiveness is the flexibility needed

to allow both of you to grow through the inevitable bumps encountered down the road of life. Of course, if your spouse does not apologize, or follows an insincere "I'm sorry" with the same old abusive behavior, then your marriage is in serious trouble and needs counseling.

4. **DATE**: Along with forgetting to talk, married couples often forget to date. Again, the excuse of a busy schedule allows for romance to be squeezed out of the marriage, and, being starved for attention, it begins to die. Dating need not mean spending a bundle at a fancy restaurant. A pizza out or a video in are just fine. Work as hard on your marriage as you do on your career, remembering to keep romance alive with cards, flowers, holding hands, and the hugs and kisses that were the hallmark of your early relationship.

5. **PRAY**: Many couples get lost in our materialistic culture, which preaches that money buys happiness, compelling them to push each other up an endless, stress-filled ladder towards a goal that is always just out of reach. Knowing what really matters will provide you with the breadcrumbs needed to find your way through the often-confusing forest of life, guiding you to true and lasting happiness.

5. Warning: Marriage in Trouble!

QUESTION: The divorce rate scares me. My wife and I have been married for 10 years, but all our friends are splitting up. What are some of the warning signs of a marriage in trouble?

ANSWER

Your question is good, but your focus is bad. Let's not only look at what is wrong, but also at what to do to make it right, as "prevention is worth a pound of cure".

Imagine that you have only given lip service to the advice that has been given, a troubled marriage as well as the road to hell being paved with good intentions. Now, being married for 10 years, you begin to sense that your marriage is in trouble. Wanting more than an intuitive sense that things may be going awry, what are some of the warning signs for which you might look?

1. **BEING TOO INDEPENDENT**: It's boring being married to Superman. He doesn't need anyone. As no man is an island, learn to love yourself enough to ask for help.

2. **BEING SELFISH**: Love is not competition. If you do not give, then you will not receive. Unless you feed the emotional needs of your spouse, he or she will starve, and be unwilling to feed you.

3. **BEING JEALOUS**: Love is a quality, not a quantity. The time given by your spouse to your children, parents and friends does not decrease what you get; it only increases his or her ability to love you all the more.

4. **BEING VENGEFUL**: As your goal is intimacy instead of victory, holding grudges or throwing a litany of past mistakes at your spouse only pushes them away from you. Giving them another chance to grow gives *you* another chance to be loved.

5. **BEING SECRETIVE**: The goal is to be one, not two. Not sharing your worries and whereabouts erodes trust. Separating income and bills into "his" and "her" piles leads to separate lives.

6. **NOT TALKING**: Being too busy to talk means a growing chasm filled with alienation and loneliness. Giving a little time to each other now will save you from spending a lot of time and money later with a divorce lawyer.

7. **NOT CHOOSING**: Trying to simultaneously please your mother and your spouse gets you stuck in the middle. Put your spouse first, and they will put you first.

8. **NOT FLEXIBLE**: Rigidly forcing the "same old, same old" down your spouse's throat may win the battle, but you will lose the war. Loosen up, and realize that there are two sides to any argument, and that surprisingly *you* may just be wrong!

9. **NOT ROMANTIC**: When was the last time that you gave your spouse flowers, took them out to dinner, or told them that you love them? Hold hands, and give each other a hug and kiss. A little effort will give you a big result!

10. **NOT PRAYING**: The old saying "the family that prays together stays together" points to our need for spiritual insight in a world blinded by secularism. Go to church or synagogue, not because you have to, but because it offers you support both personally and as a couple.

6. Trial Marriages

QUESTION: Given the high percentage of divorces today, my boyfriend and I want to know what's wrong with living together before tying the knot? Why can't the church okay that?

ANSWER

The main reason is that the church does not want you to get hurt. Let me explain with four comments.

First, while there is a world of difference between "living together" and "having a fling", **the danger of being emotionally hurt** exists when two different levels of commitment come crashing together. For one person a relationship may mean giving heart and soul, whereas for the other it may imply a convenient arrangement, perhaps ending when a company transfer occurs. Half a commitment still results in a full measure of pain.

Secondly, there is no such thing as a trial marriage. Only couples who exchange unconditional vows with one another can truly experience what marriage is like. I have seen countless couples who have lived together for years, and who, upon feeling that it is safe to marry, discover to their amazement that they have entered a new dimension. No longer can he join every sports league under the sun, nor can she come home at 4 AM after a night out with the girls. Sharing feelings is expected rather than sheepishly requested, using as their rationale "we're married now".

Thirdly, marriage is a lot more than "tying the knot". This implies a legal contract instead of a loving relationship. It implies losing freedom for personal pursuits instead of gaining freedom for interpersonal intimacy. And it implies being tied to one person until boredom inevitably and insidiously develops instead of embarking on a mutual journey that is incredibly complex and exciting.

Fourthly, for those who are religious, **marriage is a sacrament**, a sign of the unconditional love that God has for us. How confusing it would be to have the church endorse conditional and time-limited relationships outside of marriage. If it becomes okay to limit our love for one another, might we not slip into limiting our love for God, or wondering if the love of God for us is equally limited?

So, while I recognize that many people live together today, I am not sure that makes it okay. If you are scared of commitment, let us help you to prepare for marriage. But let us not lose sight of the forest for the trees, becoming blinded by societal pressure to the illumination of a sacrament.

7. Why Go to Weddings?

QUESTION: I go to the church for a wedding because I'd be embarrassed to only show up at the reception. Why go to weddings? No offense, but aren't they kind of boring?

ANSWER

When, I read the question from this person, I thought to myself: "Gee, it must have been a thrill having such a party pooper dusting off a pew at the wedding." But, all kidding aside, when you get an invitation to a wedding, do you groan at the thought of having to sit through a boring ceremony before feeling entitled to go to the reception where all the fun is? Well, if that is what you secretly think, thanks for being honest, and now let us look at why it is important for you to go to the wedding.

1. **WHAT IS MARRIAGE?** Why do people marry? If it is simply because they are lonely, or want to put 2 incomes together for a better life, then they are two individuals living at the same address, but not really married.

- Marriage is defined, whether you think in terms of theology, philosophy, sociology, or law, as the consent that a couple makes to one another on their wedding day, the "I DO" that is the heart of the ceremony.

- This consent, this marital vow, is not a boring, stagnant legal contract carved in stone that reduces their freedom by locking them into a relationship.

- No. Instead, it is a living, breathing commitment to ongoing growth with one another. As I said above, it is a protective bubble surrounding the couple, keeping interference out and intimacy in, thereby giving their relationship enough power to help each other grow to become more fully who they are meant to be, no matter what life may have in store for them.

2. **WHY HAVE A WEDDING?** The reason that you should come to the wedding ceremony is to experience a double gift: one for the couple and one for you.

a. ***A Gift for Them***: As life has more than a few bumps built into it, you are there to offer your support to your friends whenever they might hit a rough time in their marriage. Just as they are committed to each other, you are committed to them, not out of duty, but out of love. They will receive a number of gifts on their wedding day, but the main one that will not rust or fade, or end up at the back of a closet collecting dust, is your love.

b. *A Gift for You*: But wait, there is also a gift for you! The reason that marriage is a *sacrament* is that marriage is a *sign* of how much God loves you. We cannot see God, and hence, we need sacraments or signs to help us see in the material world what we cannot see in the spiritual one.

- If you ever wondered whether God loved you, take a long hard look at the couple being married. While they are nervous, they also are very much in love. You can see it in how they talk about and look at each other.

- God loves you as deeply as that. If you were to stand at the Pearly Gates today and worry if you would gain entry into heaven, and then discovered that your spouse was on the other side and could decide whether or not you get in, you would probably relax instantly, as you know he or she would immediately admit you. Why? Because they love you.

- Well, God loves you that much and more. So, when your cynical self leaves the church, and when doubt inevitably creeps into your soul as to whether God really cares, remember the love you saw between your friends at their wedding. Relish the gift they gave you: knowing that God loves you very, very much!

OUR MAP: *Loving Your Spouse*

PRINCIPLES and PROBLEMS
How our principles helped solve these problems.

<u>INSECURITY</u>: Marry a person humble and honest enough to admit their insecurity.

<u>POWER</u>: While external looks attract us, love develops when endearing internal qualities are perceived.

<u>SUCCESS</u>: Do not sacrifice your marriage for your job.

FURTHER READING

- Baer, Greg, <u>Real Love in Marriage: The Truth About Finding Genuine Happiness Now and Forever</u>, New York, Gotham Books, 2006.
- Bloom, Linda and Charlie, <u>101 Things I Wish I Knew When I Got Married</u>, Novato, CA, New World Library, 2004.
- Fortel, Mort, <u>Marriage Fitness: 4 Steps to Building & Maintaining Phenomenal Love</u>, Baltimore, MD, Marriage Max, 2004.
- Halford, W. Kim, <u>Brief Therapy for Couples: Helping Partners Help Themselves</u>, New York, Guilford Press, 2003.
- Isaacson, Cliff and Meg Schneider, <u>The Good-for-You Marriage: How a Better Marriage Can Improve Your Health, Prolong Your Life, and Ensure Your Happiness</u>, Avon, MA, Adams Media, 2008.
- Larson, Jeffrey H., <u>The Great Marriage Tune-Up Book</u>, San Francisco, Jossey-Bass, 2003.
- Mikulincer, Mario, and Gail S. Goodman, Eds., <u>Dynamics of Romantic Love: Attachment, Caregiving and Sex</u>, New York, Guilford Press, 2006.

C. Loving Your Children

1. Five Forms of Parenting

QUESTION: Are there basic types of parenting that are good or bad? I mean, what is healthy parenting?

ANSWER

Over the years I have been able to distinguish five forms of parenting; the first four are bad, the last good.

1. **NEGLECTFUL/ABUSIVE PARENTING**: Some parents, having difficulty being loved by adults, see children as a safe way to receive all the love that they want. When such unrealistic expectations collide with cries around the clock for feedings and diaper changes, this overly insecure person could allow anger to escalate from neglect to abuse.

2. **OVERPROTECTIVE PARENTING**: The anxious parent who runs out the back door to settle every childish squabble or who daily walks their eighth grader to school unwittingly communicates a sense of weakness in the child, who gradually becomes more scared of doing things independently.

3. **OVERCRITICAL PARENTING**: Wanting a child to succeed may lead to pushing the child too hard, conveying the message that love is conditional upon getting an A, hitting a home run, or making varsity cheerleading.

4. **OVERPERMISSIVE PARENTING**: Not wanting to hamper the creativity of the child, or perhaps fearing that firm rules may cause the child to reject the parent, some parents give children an alarming sense of power. Not having to suffer normal consequences, the child may feel entitled to favors, exploit friends, or become a discipline problem.

5. **HEALTHY PARENTING**: This is essentially the opposite of the first four. Parents should be caring instead of neglectful, promote autonomy instead of dependence, provide unconditional instead of conditional love, and set realistic limits and guidelines.

Finally, we need to mix in a pinch of common sense to my ingredients. What makes 1-4 unhealthy is that they are patterns, namely, that the mistakes are consistently repeated. We all make the occasional blunder, but as long as we generally hit the mark, all should be well.

Now, let us look in more detail at the three forms of problem parenting that I most commonly see in my office: overprotective, overcritical and overpermissive.

2. Overprotective Parenting

QUESTION: *My husband says that I'm overprotective with our son. In this scary world, is there really such a thing as being too protective?*

ANSWER

When is too much protection too much? When your child begins to feel weak. To make my point, let me describe what overprotective parenting would look like for your son.

While you may be an anxious, first-time parent, your son only knows that the way you treat him is different from all his friends. He goes to bed earlier than they do. You come out and rescue him from a minor tiff at the swings. You tie his shoes for him or dress him in the morning to his consternation with his sleep-over friend watching, giggling, and waiting to call him "a baby".

Later, you dissuade him from trying out for football as he is "thin-boned", and from asking a girl to the dance because he cried when a girl said no the last time. When he considers a college away from home, you tell him how he hated camp, and urge him to find a local school. When he goes to marry, you imply that he is naïve and being controlled by his fiancée.

What overprotective parenting says, therefore, is "You're just not strong enough to handle this". Repeated often enough, your child is conditioned to begin believing that message. Now, I realize that you do not mean to convey that message, but that is definitely what your child hears.

So, protect your child, but not at the expense of his autonomy. Trust in your own training. Your son is smart, has absorbed your teaching, and will do just fine. If he goofs, don't panic. Just help him to think through what went wrong, and establish a new game plan. Giving him some headroom and helping him think for himself demonstrates your confidence and trust in him. Doing it for him, or suggesting he not try, unwittingly produces a follower, not a leader. Is that what you really want?

KEY POINTS

- Overprotective Parenting tells your child that he is weak.
- Protect your child, but not at the expense of his feeling strong and self-confident.

3. Overcritical Parenting

QUESTION: My wife tells me that I'm too harsh with our kids. When I was grow-ing up, my dad was a lot more than harsh, pushing me all the time to work hard and giving me a good swift kick in the butt when I didn't. Life is hard. What's wrong with preparing kids for what they're going to find out there in the real world when they leave home?

ANSWER

Helping your child to prepare for the demands that life inevitably makes is a tremendous gift that a parent can offer a child. But portraying life in a cynical way tarnishes your gift, and delivering that message in a harsh manner confuses the child, making them wonder whether their value and your love are condi-tional upon performance.

While you want your son or daughter to live up to their potential, you do not want them to sweat buckets when they come home with an F in spelling in 4th Grade, fearing that you may revoke their membership card to the family. They need to know that you want them to do their best, but that your love is unconditional. Win or lose, you will be there for them.

It is important that you teach that distinction now, for if you do not, they may later internalize the formula of inner worth being predicated upon outer performance and forever have an overcritical monkey on their backs. As kids, the examples are easy enough to spot; all you need do is watch their reaction to disappointments, such as not getting a hit in a Little League game, getting a C instead of an A in math, not making the football team in high school, not mak-ing the honor roll, and so forth.

Your response to their reaction will be key. If you are critical, scolding them for "goofing off" or labeling them "a loser" who will "never amount to any-thing if you keep this up", you are reinforcing the negative message with which they have already branded themselves. When they leave home, your role in this process will end, but they will be running for the rest of their lives to prove themselves through a better job, a higher salary, a lower golf handicap, a better neighborhood, or whatever bespeaks success to them.

By not only sharing their disappointment, but also reassuring them of your love and encouraging them to try harder the next time, you mirror for them their value, and make them realize that tomorrow is, after all, another day. As their value is within them, then a loss today does not a loser make. Their innate abilities will rise to the occasion the next time, the pain of the disparity today between one's inner potential and outer mistake being countered by another at bat tomorrow that will most probably yield a different result.

So, prepare your child for life, but do so with understanding and love, and without harshness and cynicism.

A True Story

Let me end with a true story about a thirteen-year old boy, as it will make clear the harm that an overcritical parent can inflict on a child. The boy is in seventh grade, and has made one of the teams in Babe Ruth baseball, which is open to boys from the seventh to the ninth grade. His team has had a good season, and has made it to the league championship game. As he is in seventh grade, and as there is a considerable difference in the strength of boys between the seventh and ninth grades, the coach plays the older boys. The boy understands, and sits on the bench enthusiastically rooting for his team.

By the fifth inning, his team is ahead by four runs, and so the coach decides to put the younger boys into the game, sending him to right field. He is ecstatic, knowing that very few balls are hit to right field, and the chances of making a big mistake are small.

But gradually the other team catches up, now being only one run behind his team. It is the bottom of the ninth inning, the other team is at bat, there are two outs, the bases are loaded, and their big hitter is at the plate. Our boy is nervously praying for either a strikeout or a hit that goes anywhere but near him.

Crack! A long fly ball is hit over his head in right field. He races back and leaps in the air, catching the ball, but awkwardly falling backwards as he was off balance. Somehow, he has the presence of mind to hold onto the ball, and raises his mitt to show to all that he has caught the ball to end the game. His teammates know that he has saved the day, and rush out to hoist him onto their shoulders and carry him off the field.

He is the hero of the game! The local newspaper is there to take his picture, and everyone is cheering. Everyone, that is, except his parents, as his mother is not interested in sports, and his father is an older man, tired, and has never come to any of his games. The boy cannot wait to tell his father.

He races home on his bike, drops it by the side door of the house, excitedly running into the house where he finds his father in the den smoking a cigar and reading the evening paper. The boy hurriedly tells his father the story, who pauses to listen to his son. When the boy is finished, the father asks, "Did you get a hit?" When the boy says no, the father acts disgusted, dismissing his son with a cursory wave of his arm. The boy runs upstairs with tears in his eyes, throws his mitt against the wall, and yells, "I hate my father".

Can you imagine how the boy must have felt? He thinks that he just does not measure up, and so either gives up and further shrinks in self-confidence, or decides to aggressively do whatever it takes to please his father. Either way, he is a tortured soul, and the only way that he will heal will be to take back the power to determine his worth. Of course, that will not realistically occur until he is much older, and so the continual criticism of what he does will deepen his doubt in himself and anger at his father, or any authority figure for whom he must perform to please. Was that the intent of the father? Maybe not, but that was the impact on the boy.

KEY POINTS

- Overcritical Parenting tells your child that
  - o he does not measure up, and that
  - o your love is conditional upon his performance.
- It's OK to set goals, but when they are not met,
  - o share your child's disappointment instead of scolding him, and
  - o reassure him of your love and support instead of being on his back to perform.

4. Overpermissive Parenting

QUESTION: *My brother and his wife let their kids get away with murder. A 6-year old who goes to bed at 11 PM, swear words that are excused as "expressing themselves" or "getting their anger out", have made my nephew and niece brats. However, when I try to talk to my brother and sister-in-law, I come across as "mean". If I'm right, how do I get my message across?*

ANSWER: Here are two points to consider.

1. **THEIR BOUNDARIES**:
   a. **The Cause**: The reasons for not setting clear boundaries may be many.
      i.   Perhaps your brother and sister-in-law both work, get home late, and want to spend more time with their children.
      ii. Or, maybe they have such little time with them, they do not want to use that time fighting with their children about going to bed, or may fear that setting clear limits may mar their images of being nurturing and loving.
      iii. They may also want to counter what they themselves experienced growing up as repressive by allowing their own children to be more expressive.
   b. **The Result**: The problem is that your brother and sister-in-law may be unwittingly crossing the boundary line between constructive and destructive freedom. The former encourages a child to attempt sailing into the lands of creativity and autonomy, but with the foreknowledge that parents are watching and guiding the journey. The latter removes too much of the safety net underneath these flights, causing children to either unnecessarily be hurt or labeled.

      Expressing one's self is great, but telling a teacher that he or she is "an asshole", skipping school due to a fake tummy ache, experimenting with what a coke poured over a laptop computer will do, or threatening a temper tantrum if they do not get the expensive present they want, can get them into a world of trouble and labeled by their uncle as "brats".

2. <u>**YOUR MESSAGE**</u>:

Dragging me into the argument with your brother and sister-in-law to bolster your case will only further alienate you from them, and get them so defensive as to be unable to hear what you are trying to say. Instead, help them to consider what they really want and their kids really need.

As regards what they really want, it is time with and love from their children. There are more creative ways than allowing a 6-year old to stay up until 11 PM, the grumpy, next-day behavior from an overtired child being an indication that more quality time on the weekend than guilty time on a weeknight might be the answer.

As regards the needs of their children, not setting guidelines is actually hurting rather than loving their kids, making their children think that being disrespectful is somehow permissible, and giving their children the insecure feeling that they are running the show instead of their parents. Will your brother and sister-in-law lose their children's love? No. Will they gain their respect? Yes.

5. Discipline

QUESTION: My friends allow their kids to rule the roost. When these darlings disobey their parents and get into trouble, the parents sit them down to "reason with them", when I think a good spanking would do wonders. Don't you think I'm right?

ANSWER

Many parents still cling to the notion that a good spanking now and then does a world of good. The trouble with a spanking is that when the sting of the swat stops, so too does the child's thinking about his or her disobedience. Not understanding why what they did was wrong, the child may feel like the victim, and simply learn to become better at hiding, waiting until parents are out of sight, or perhaps lying to them if they become suspicious.

An alternative to becoming the neighborhood James Bond is for the child to become shy and withdrawn. Assuming that his own behavior gets him into trouble, he may become an expert in guessing, "what Mommy wants me to do". While this seems to produce the "model child", the child in actuality doubts his or her own autonomy, and grows up thinking that being loved is conditional upon playing the game according to someone else's rules. Even if successful, the child doubts his own worth, and resents constantly putting his own desires in second place.

How then does a parent discipline? The obvious trick is to gain obedience without losing autonomy. Your friends are on the right track, as the goal is to help the child to think, teaching a child to talk out his behavior, making him responsible for his behavior both by consciously making him choose it, and then making him accept the consequences of his choice.

Making the child choose his behavior involves making the choice very clear, both in terms of the behaviors involved and their consequences. Not eating spinach means Sally loses desert, and not going to bed on time tonight means Steve will have to go a half-hour earlier for the next two nights. When the child protests by either whining or throwing a temper tantrum, the parent must enforce the negative consequences in a calm and consistent manner, reminding the child that the choice was his.

The dynamics for older children are the same, simply involving a longer and more sophisticated discussion. While the value of a balanced meal or a good night's rest is hard to debate, what time your teenage daughter comes home from a date is not quite so clear. The concerns of both the adolescent and parents need to be shared, alternative solutions brainstormed, and a decision with consequences chosen. So, if parents decide to trust Mary with an 11 PM curfew, and she comes home at midnight drunk, not only should the consequences previously decided upon be enforced, but also another discussion should occur to go over why her parents are so upset, and how she could have handled that situation more like an adult.

A few final remarks are that the punishment should be meaningful. Sending Mike to his room may not mean much if he has a television, CD player, computer, comics and toys there. Believe it or not, let the child propose his own punishment as this increases his sense of responsibility and decreases his picture of you as Adolf Hitler's clone. Also, calm down before talking, as losing your temper, calling your child "stupid", and imposing unrealistic punishments will damage both your relationship with your child and his self-image, not to mention having you rescind your punishment and thereby look inconsistent.

So, remember reasoning with your child rather than striking him will produce a reasonable adult rather than an angry rebel or a compliant martyr.

KEY POINTS

- **Spankings**
  - o may not promote thinking, but
  - o may promote a child who feels like a victim and so
    - manipulates and lies, or
    - becomes shy, withdrawn and overly compliant.
- **Talking**
  - o promotes thinking about why something was wrong, and
  - o promotes both obedience and autonomy.
- **Help your child choose his or her own behavior, making clear,**
  - o both the behaviors involved
  - o and their consequences.

6. Single Parent Pitfalls

QUESTION: I recently became a single parent. The divorce was bad enough, but being alone while trying to raise the kids is even harder. I feel overwhelmed and I'm having a rough time. What are some pitfalls I should watch out for?

ANSWER

As the divorce rate for first marriages is high and for second marriages even higher, there are a number of parents who raise children largely alone. Co-parenting is no piece of cake, but single parenting is truly difficult. Here are some pitfalls for single parents to avoid.

1. **GUILT**: Many people feel guilty for their marriage "failing". Even if you made mistakes, forgive yourself and see your new life as just that—new. After the death of your marriage comes an opportunity to be reborn, to take a long hard look at who you are and where you are going. See it as a challenge, not a curse.

2. **GRIEF**: Work through the loss of your spouse. Let go of the desire to have your pound of flesh, face the fact that it took two to make a divorce, and try to remember that while you no longer share a marriage, you still share children and will have to work together for the rest of your life.

3. **CHILD AS SPOUSE**: If you do not work through your loss, then you may make one of two mistakes. Either you may displace anger from spouse to child, especially if the child resembles your former spouse, or you may turn your child into your spouse, wanting the emotional closeness of which divorce "robbed" you.

4. **NO COUNSELING**: Why work through it alone? See your priest, minister, rabbi, or a counselor to help you both for a re-evaluation of what went wrong in your marriage, and also for a values clarification of what you are looking for when you begin to date. If you remarry, pre-marital counseling will also help you relax in your choice and get things off on the right foot.

5. **COUPLE FRIENDS**: The death of your marriage often means the death of some friendships that both of you shared, as they often feel the need to

choose. Try not to take it personally, realize that you are about to discover who is "true blue", and see the pursuit of new friends as a new step in your new life.

6. **PUSHING FAMILY AWAY**: Let your family love you. If you need to move back home for a brief period, or need to accept financial aid, accept the love your parents and relatives want to give you. Ministering to you is growth for them.

7. **HERMITITIS**: Avoid becoming a hermit. Go to church or synagogue. Join a support group. Go out for an evening with a friend. And, while dating will probably feel like being an awkward teenager all over again, realize that Prince Charming or Cinderella are not going to come knocking on your door. You may groan at going to a singles dance, but your goal is not to be a party animal, just to gradually discover someone with whom you can share your new life.

7. The Ups and Downs Of Being A Stepparent

QUESTION: I recently remarried. I got out of a miserable marriage and hoped that life with my new wife would be so much happier. Instead, I find more ups and downs than I ever imagined. Do you have any advice for a new stepparent?

ANSWER

As one out of every two marriages ends in divorce, and as the majority of those divorced remarry, the number of reconstituted families has correspondingly risen, posing a series of ups and downs when one becomes a stepparent.

Many a stepparent dreams of entering a ready-made family where instant happiness looms just behind the door. A stepfather, for example, may expect to be called "Dad" and ushered to an oversized chair, onto which his stepchildren will climb for a hug and a bedtime story. Instead, he is greeted by children who either peek around the corner at him, or tell him to get out of their father's chair. If he tries to claim his right as their father, he may be told blatantly that he is not, and never will be, their father, and then find himself in a discipline battle over issues large and small.

Turning to his new wife for support, he may be aghast to discover that she overrules him in front of the children, telling him that her ex-husband and she always let the children stay up until midnight on weekends. Gradually, difficulty with his new stepchildren evolves into difficulty with his new wife.

The situation is often harder for a stepmother, especially if she does not work, meaning that there are larger blocks of time during which she must interact with the children. If the mother has been the first and primary source of emotional nurturance for the children, the stepmother, even if she is a direct transplant from the Brady Bunch, may be viewed as ranking three steps down from the Wicked Witch of the West.

Rather than despair, consider **three suggestions**.

1. **EXPECT A NEW NORMAL**: First, stepparents should work out new relations with stepchildren, not base "normal" on a first family, or get too upset if not called "Mom" or "Dad". The intention of the children is less to hurt you and more to remain loyal to their biological parent. Realize that you have to begin at

the beginning, getting to know your stepchildren gradually. And then both you and they must see that love is not a limited quantity to be jealously guarded, but a limitless quality to be generously bestowed, the relationships between children and their parents and stepparents being different, not competitive.

2. **TALK TOGETHER instead of ACT APART**: Secondly, spend time talking with your spouse regarding issues like discipline, rather than trying to impose old or preconceived plans on one another. What worked in the past is past, and unless you both agree on the new rules for the house, the children will see the rift and probably try to manipulate one of you against the other. This may not mean agreeing on how to discipline, but rather agreeing to let the biological parent discipline their own children, taking the pressure off the stepparent, who now simply has to support their spouse and present a united front.

3. **BE PATIENT**: Thirdly, everyone should be patient and sensitive to the adjustment being made by everyone else. The children now have to relate to two sets of parents and four sets of grandparents. A stepmother has to work to help her husband make child support payments for his children from his first marriage. A stepfather has to deal with his wife's ex-husband coming into his house every weekend to pick up the children. And then there are all the family functions and parties to which everyone is invited, making it impossible to pretend that the other marriage never existed. The point, however, is not to pretend, but to adjust, and that to adjust, you must communicate frequently with all members of this newly reconstituted family.

The stresses involved in second marriages often lead to a second divorce. So, if being hurt once was bad enough, then consider opening yourself up to the change and happiness that can be yours.

OUR MAP: *Loving Your Children*

PRINCIPLES and PROBLEMS
How our principles helped solve these problems.

INSECURITY: Help your children to learn from their mistakes rather than feel like a mistake.

POWER: Help your children see their inner worth and gradually gain autonomy.

SUCCESS: Teach your children the importance of relationships by what you do, not just what you say.

FURTHER READING

- Barber, Brian K., Intrusive Parenting: How Psychological Control Affects Children and Adolescents, Washington, D.C., American Psychological Association, 2001.

- Borba, Michele, Parents Do Make a Difference: How to Raise Kids with Solid Character, Strong Minds, and Caring Hearts, San Francisco, Jossey-Bass, 1999.

- Christophersen, Edward R., and Susan L. Mortweet, Parenting That Works: Building Skills that Last a Lifetime, Washington, D.C., American Psychological Association, 2002.

- Gilbert, Roberta M., Connecting with Our Children: Guiding Principles for Parents in a Troubled World, New York, John Wiley & Sons, 1999.

- Popkin, Michael, and Robyn Freedman Spizman, Getting Through to Your Kids, New York, Pedigree Book, 2002.

- Taffel, Ron, and Roberta Israeloff, When Parents Disagree and What You Can Do About It, New York, Guilford Press, 2002.

CHAPTER THREE

CHALLENGES ALONG THE WAY

Much like Dorothy traveling down the Yellow Brick Road to see the Wizard of Oz, we all encounter challenges along the way during our lifetime. Whether big or small, they can shift your growth either up or down, derail your progress or be an opportunity for a quantum leap forward to deeper maturity and happiness.

We shall look at some of the most common ones that all of us encounter, such as stress, work, illness and death, and even holidays like Thanksgiving, Christmas and New Year's.

A. Stress

1. Sixteen Ways to Cope with Stress

QUESTION: Lately, I feel like I'm drowning in stress. Do you have any practical suggestions that I could use?

ANSWER

Stress is a fact of life. The world is a busy place in which we work hard to meet deadlines and make promotions, and to be assertive with the spouse who does not listen or the store that overcharges and underserves. Therefore, instead of kidding ourselves that we can avoid stress, we must understand ways to cope with it. Here is a quick look at sixteen ways.

1. **Recognize the Signs of Stress**: The sooner you spot the signs, the sooner you can stop the stress. Common signs are a pounding heart, sweaty palms and brow, tension at the back of your neck or in the pit of your stomach, a headache (often the feeling of a tight band across your forehead), a back-ache, irritability, pacing the floor, wringing your hands, and fatigue.

2. **Determine Priorities**: You cannot do it all. So, learn to do a few things well, instead of many poorly.

3. **Drop Unrealistic Expectations**: Drop excessive use of words like "must" and "should" from your vocabulary. Pick up words like "no" and recognize your limits. Not being 150% involved does not mean being lazy.

4. **Talk to Yourself**: Analyze whether your thinking is dominated by ideas that filter out your positives and accentuate your negatives, blowing out of proportion mistakes which you may have made.

5. **Talk to Others**: Express instead of suppress your feelings. Be assertive and sensitive instead of being an explosive volcano or someone who silently seethes, until the inevitable sarcastic snipe oozes out on the victim.

6. **Give in Once in a While**: Make allowances for the fact that you could be wrong; avoid being obstinate and defiant.

7. **Tackle One Task at a Time**: Deal with the most urgent tasks first; partialize the big loads, remembering the old joke, "How do you eat an elephant? One bite at a time."

8. **Take a Breather**: Five minutes "off" can lead to most of your day being "on". Take a walk or just step away from your desk, instead of making yourself "stand there and suffer".

9. **Deep Breathing**: A simple relaxation exercise is to sit still for a few minutes and breathe deeply, not so dramatic that anyone can notice, just so that you feel more relaxed and under control.

10. **Meditation**: Deep breathing can be combined with focusing upon one idea or object so as to slow your mind down and give your body a rest. It will also make you more productive when you return to work, as increasing your focus will decrease your sense of being too scattered.

11. **Join a Support Group**: If your extended family is geographically distant, try to make friends with whom you can be yourself, or join a support group, whether at your church, synagogue, or civic group. Even a men's group at a golf club or bowling league can help relieve some stress by giving you relaxation as well as friends.

12. **Exercise to Relax**: A routine of walking, jogging, or any regular exercise program can work off pent-up frustration. If you are able to, try to alternate between weight-bearing and aerobic exercises, always after preliminary stretching exercises.

13. **Massage**: A regular massage may be too expensive, but consider treating yourself to a massage when under a great deal of stress. If you are married, asking your spouse for a massage not only soothes aching muscles, but also provides a time of romance and intimacy, let alone saving money!

14. **Try Helping Others**: Focusing on the troubles of others may put yours in perspective.

15. **Develop a Hobby**: A new interest can get your mind off an old problem; woodwork, kite flying, gardening, stamp collecting—whatever you like.

16. **Pray**: I saved the best for last. Try daily prayer, meditation, or reading scripture to show you the meaning of your life. This can be combined with some of the above. For instance, you can read scripture for five minutes, and then meditate on the meaning of what you read for another five minutes, breathing deeply while doing so. Not only are you learning to relax, but you are learning how to focus on one thing at a time instead of ruminating over many.

2. Back to School:
Back to Being Overloaded?

QUESTION: *Oh God, the kids are going back to school, and schlepping them from activity to activity has always made them and me absolutely overloaded! But, if I don't make sure that they take advantage of every opportunity, I fear that they may squander their youth and pay for it for the rest of their lives. Do you have any suggestions as to how I can deal with the pressures of parenting?*

ANSWER

Entry into another school year often means tighter and more hectic schedules for both parent and child, the kids adding numerous extracurricular activities to a full day of classes, and parents feeling like they are "endlessly schlepping them from one activity to another". Being back in school should not mean being back to being overloaded, and so here are some thoughts to consider.

1. <u>**STRESS IN MY CHILD?**</u> Are you pushing your child too hard? Some parents, with the best of intentions, may unwittingly overschedule their children in the hope of giving them an edge over their peers in our competitive society. Sadly, one out of three children suffers from stress-related illnesses.

2. <u>**SIGNS OF OVERLOAD**</u>: The goal is not to avoid structured time, but rather to not overdo it. Here are some behavioral signs of overload: physical symptoms (headache, stomachache), being tired and falling asleep in class, being irritable and agitated, grades dropping, cheating on tests, less interest in activities, preferring to stay home and being more dependent on you.

3. <u>**SOLUTIONS**</u>:
   a. *<u>Find a Balance</u>*: Limit the number of activities, providing time to play and just "be a kid".
   b. *<u>Realize the Benefits of Play</u>*: Having time to play encourages creativity and independent problem solving, improves social skills, and relieves stress.

c.   ***Take a Day of Rest***: Make one day per week free of activities, giving you and your children a well-deserved break—sort of a non-religious Sabbath.

d.   ***Choose Gifted Programs that are Gifted***: More work, but less creativity, will make matters worse.

e.   ***Choose Sports that Build Self-Esteem***: While teaching teamwork and cooperation are fine, equating worth with performance, and having a coach or teammates who berate your child are not. Ask your child the simple question, "Are you having fun?"

f.   ***Examine Yourself***: Is your child overloaded because you are overloaded? Consider escaping pressure yourself rather than feeding it to your child. Being pushed to be the smartest, most athletic, fashionable, thin and popular kid in the class has been shown to push kids away from being happy. Perhaps examining your own view of life might help.

3. Clergy Stress: Myth or Reality?

QUESTION: Last week, our Pastor told us that he was feeling "stressed out" and overwhelmed by his work. Everyone was shocked. Shouldn't he have it altogether? Is stress really a factor for clergy?

ANSWER

Another issue about stress may surprise you, namely, that clergy have stress. The myth that clergy have an easy time of it is just that—a myth! Clergy are quite susceptible to stress for a wide variety of reasons. Here are six:

1. **Expectations**: As so many clergy apply for each congregation, the search committee begins to think that they should get a stirring preacher, a scholarly theologian, a vibrant youth leader, an insightful counselor, and an administrative whiz. Should the minister or rabbi attempt to be all things to all people, the "S" on his or her chest will be for "stress", not "superman".

2. **Projections**: In a similar vein, people may project an idealized person on the pastor, hoping for the perfect parent or spouse. The love a person in the congregation did not get in the past is now expected to be magically replaced by the pastor. When the pastor proves to have feet of clay, irrational but nonetheless hurtful anger is directed at him or her, usually disguised as criticism of "simply not measuring up".

3. **Work Overload**: Your pastor is literally on call 24 hours a day. This does not mean that they should not have two days off each week, nor does it imply that they should not be assertive about "emergency" calls that are anything but emergencies. It does imply that no minister or rabbi has a 40-hour week, and that as the congregation grows, so too should the role of the laity. While it may be hard for some clergy to let others help them, perhaps fearing criticism if they do so, we need to remember that even Moses got asked to delegate work by Joshua, and that it was no accident that Jesus had 12 apostles.

4. **Role Confusion**: The role of a pastor has changed over time. Gone are the days when the image of the Church being the center of the town was accurate. Today, clergy are missionaries in a militantly secular society, sailing

out in their cars to evangelize the world. This shift means going out instead of waiting for people to come in, and some clergy, let alone some congregations, have trouble adjusting to a mission rather than maintenance model.

5. **Marital Conflict**: A study a few years ago showed that 60% of clergy spouses were angry at always being in second place to the congregation, wanting their spouses to set clearer limits to unrealistic demands, and to be more assertive about a needed raise in salary or repair to their home if supplied by the congregation.

6. **Metaphors for Ministry**: A final note is that the very images we have for our pastor often work against him or her. Being the "caregiver" or the "suffering servant" makes it hard to then ask for help and be the "caregivee".

So, consider giving your pastor the gift that keeps on giving, yourself. Let him or her know that you care, show them that you understand, and encourage them to let you help.

OUR MAP: *Stress*

PRINCIPLES and PROBLEMS
How our principles helped solve these problems.

<u>INSECURITY</u>: Relax—no one can do it all.

<u>POWER</u>: Drop the pressure of others that you "should" please and perform, and pick up the ability to assert your limits by saying "no".

<u>SUCCESS</u>: Focus less on the amount of work being done, and more on your growth while working (your creativity, integrity, responsibility, etc.).

FURTHER READING

- Davis, Martha, Elizabeth Robbins Eschelman, and Matthew McKay, <u>The Relaxation & Stress Reduction Workbook</u>, 5th Ed., Oakland, CA, New Harbinger Publications, 2000.

- Luskin, Fred, and Kenneth R. Pelletier, <u>Stress Free for Good: 10 Scientifically Proven Life Skills for Health & Happiness</u>, San Francisco, Harper, 2005.

- Marks, David Ryan, <u>Raising Stable Kids in an Unstable World: A Physician's Guide to Dealing with Childhood Stress</u>, Deerfield Beach, FL, Health Communications, Inc., 2002.

- Oswald, Roy M., <u>Clergy Self-Care: Finding a Balance for Effective Ministry</u>, Washington, D.C., The Alban Institute, 1991.

B. Work

QUESTION: I've been unemployed for almost a year now. I'm trying, but I just can't find a job. I'm so embarrassed. For a while I even pretended to go to work so none of the neighbors would know. I feel like such a loser!

ANSWER

The problem of this person, and of our culture, is that we define ourselves not by **who we are**, but by **what we do**. If we "do more" than others, as evidenced by an impressive job title or a big salary, then we feel important. By contrast, if we "do less" than others, or "do nothing" by virtue of being unemployed, then we feel unimportant and depressed.

Depression, which we shall discuss in more detail later, is a gap between our ego ("who we are") and our ego ideal ("who we think we should be"). If you think that you should be at the top of the corporate ladder, or at least competitively clawing your way up the ladder, then, being too low on the ladder or out of a job, you fall into the gap and get depressed. The solution is to drop the "shoulds" and "musts" that are strangling you, and to come to love and accept the person underneath all your accomplishments.

Who you are is more important than the sum of what you do. Who you are defines your potential or power to do. Within you is a mind with which to think, a heart with which to love, an imagination with which to dream, and qualities such as honesty, integrity, and kindness that attract people to you. Ask your family why they love you; I doubt that it is because you have or had a great job.

Changing the way you think will, therefore, take a monkey off your back. The old you said, "I do good things; therefore, I am good." This way you are always nervous, waiting for the other shoe to drop, for someone to notice your first mistake and proclaim, "Aha, a loser".

However, the new you says, "I am good; therefore, I have the ability to do good things." This way, even if you goof, you do not panic, but resolve to do better tomorrow. Amazingly, as you are less worried regarding criticism, you become even more productive than in the past.

So, while the fact that you may someday be unemployed is bad, **you** are not! You are just as talented as ever. If others cannot see this truth because they are lost in the same forest that you once were, then try to help them, but do not allow yourself to get sucked back into their way of thinking. And, hard as it is, try to see that while other factors such as a recessionary economy and possible age (or sex, or race) discrimination may hurt you, they are not due to anything wrong with you. Bad as it is, unemployment can have a good effect, awakening you to see your own value, and allowing you to minister to others caught in the same trap.

OUR MAP: *Work*

PRINCIPLES and PROBLEMS
How our principles helped solve these problems.

<u>SUCCESS</u>: Your worth is predicated upon **who** you are more than **what** you do.
- You are not a failure if you make mistakes.
- You are not less because of doing less if unemployed.

FURTHER READING

- Bhagat, Rabi S. and James C. Segoris, <u>Work, Stress and Coping in an Era of Globalization</u>, Mahwah, NJ, Lawrence Erlbaum Associates, 2007.

- Jaeger, Barrie S., <u>Making Work Work for the Highly Sensitive Person</u>, New York, McGraw Hill, 2005.

- Warr, Peter, <u>Work, Happiness and Unhappiness</u>, Mahwah, NJ, Lawrence Erlbaum Associates, 2007.

C. The Middle-Age Crisis

QUESTION: What happens to some people when they turn 40? My brother-in-law dumped my sister, telling her that she'd held him back. Now he's living with a much younger woman. Why do some middle-age men act like such asses?

ANSWER

We have all seen a man whose behavior changes wildly, divorcing his wife, moving in with a much younger woman, suddenly dropping those extra pounds and picking up a hair piece, wearing a gold chain and driving a Corvette. Why?

Middle age becomes a crisis when we fear that life is a lost opportunity, that our chance to be happy is slipping through our fingers like sand.

Many assume that by 40 success should be firmly within their grasp. When it is not, some turn the blame out, typically blaming their spouse for such things as not letting them take that new job because it meant moving the family. So, they have an affair, get a divorce, and find someone who will hopefully be more supportive. Many also project blame to their boss, telling him or her off, quitting their job, hoping to find a new career that will finally be the key to their success.

Yet, turning the blame out will eventually prove to be a flop. Life with a second wife will not prove to be much different, and his new career will show no signs of making him a tycoon.

The real solution to this unbelievable mess is amazingly simple. Remember one of our core thoughts at the beginning of the book. Happiness is not a goal reached at age 40; it is a process throughout our lives. People should not panic because they do not have a monopoly on happiness at 40. No one does!

For the victim of a middle-age crisis, the shock is that real happiness has been under his nose all along. The man about whom we have been talking could be married for 50 years and only have scratched the surface of what true intimacy can attain. Instead of looking outside of himself to a new wife, a new job, a sports car and a hairpiece, he should look within himself and really face the issue of the meaning of his life.

Middle age should not, therefore, be a crisis, but a challenge. We are each an explorer, peering through the trees at a beautiful valley that will take a lifetime to explore. Take joy in the reality that there is always more happiness just around the corner, no matter how old we are.

OUR MAP: *The Middle-Age Crisis*

PRINCIPLES and PROBLEMS
How our principles helped solve these problems.

INSECURITY: Perfection is not a race ending at 40, but a process of growth ending at death.

SUCCESS: Being successful is not having a big car by the middle of your life, but a big soul at the end of your life.

FURTHER READING

- Hollis, James, Finding Meaning in the Second Half of Life: How to Finally Grow Up, New York, Gotham Books, 2005.
- Johnson, Robert A., and Jerry M. Ruhl, Living Your Unlived Life: Coping with Unrealized Dreams & Fulfilling Your Purpose in the Second Half of Life, New York, Jeremy P. Tarcher/Penguin Group, 2007.
- Sellers, Ronnie, Ed., Fifty Things To Do When You Turn Fifty, Portland, Maine, Sellers Publishing, 2005.

D. Old Age

1. Old and Useless

QUESTION: I am growing old. As I am less able to do things, and as retirement is just around the corner, I am feeling increasingly old and useless. My wife tells me that I'm too negative and have the wrong "perspective". Is she right?

ANSWER

This gentleman knew that his wife was right, but did not have a mental framework with which to understand and change his behavior. Here are some of the things that I told him.

1. **PERSPECTIVE**: Smart wife! You view growing old as having less instead of having more. In the phrase, "growing old", you focus on "old", while your wife and I focus on "growing". In your worldview, advancing age is a problem, not an opportunity. While you focus on your physical strength decreasing, you ignore the ever-increasing growth of your mind and soul.

2. **CHANGE**: OK, I am not naively overlooking the bodily changes that progressively occur. Admittedly, your hair turns gray, and your skin becomes wrinkled and marked with liver spots. Background noise makes it harder to hear, and seeing at night is hard enough to often keep you home. The rug between your bed and the bathroom is worn thin from going back and forth at night, and waking up greets you with stiff and painful joints. Clearly, the body that used to feel like your friend increasingly feels like your enemy.

3. **CHOICE**: But, is that a reason to roll over and play dead? No! You have a choice. While you can not stop getting older, you can start dealing with it more effectively. After all, being happy does not mean being lucky in avoiding bad times, just being good at coping with them. Here are a few ways to improve coping.

    a. ***Attitude:*** While not denying the negative, try not to dwell on it. Being an optimist does not mean sticking your head in the sand, just consciously deciding to focus more on what is realistically good. Think of all that you take for granted, such as the colors of the grass and sky, the sounds of music, the smell of food or flowers, and the simple act of breathing fresh air.

b. ***Your Past***: Use the past not as a way to escape the present, but rather as a way to remember your own inner strengths and talents in coping with the present. Much of what you did in raising a family and advancing your career can be used to face rather than flee the challenges of ill health.

c. ***Your Present***: Can you grow at your age? Can you teach an old dog new tricks? Definitely. My experience has been that the elderly, knowing how precious each day is, can often grow faster than people much younger. With the philosophy of *carpe diem*, they do not waste time playing games, but more honestly face the truth.

d. ***Retirement***: One way to grow is by creatively using your retirement, viewing it not as the end of a productive life, but as a new beginning, a new expression of yourself. Think about it, as we shall spend more time in retirement than we did in school, instead of seeing ourselves as being "put out to pasture", we need new meaning in our new life. While this could be playing golf, it could also be volunteering our considerable skills to a local, non-profit organization.

e. ***Relationships***: Cutting yourself off from others makes getting stuck in negative thinking easier. Force yourself to reach out to your friends and family, people at your church or synagogue, or those at your local senior service center. And, do not underestimate the value of a pet. Having a dog enthusiastically greet you each day as a long-lost relative can be the pick-me-up that you need on a bad day.

f. ***Health Issues***:
    (1). Hearing Loss: This often leads to social withdrawal rather than facing the frustration of continually asking, "What did you say?" As the problem is typically hearing high-pitched noises, and as hearing aids tend to magnify all sounds equally, noisy settings like a restaurant or a crowded room become confusing and difficult. If this affects you, do not be shy about asking others to be more understanding, your assertiveness helping to increase the sensitivity of others let alone enabling you to be more engaged.
    (2). Vision Loss: As we age, we lose some lens transparency, so that less light gets to the retina. Accordingly, as you get older, you may have trouble seeing in dim light. Again, you will need to be assertive about

preferring to not drive at night, or asking for a ride, or requesting that the lights be turned up in a room.

(3). <u>Medication</u>: Symptoms of drowsiness, being forgetful and "slow", or unsteady of gait may often be caused not by senility, but by the need to take several drugs, the dosage of which may need to be adjusted.

g.   ***Professionals***: Find someone who will complement all that I have just said, treating you not as a problem coming to him or her for a solution, but as a person with innate strengths who is looking for someone who will be willing to enter into a collaborative and equal relationship.

2. I'm an S.O.B.

QUESTION: This letter is 40 years in the writing. I'm 79, living in a nursing home, where I have many friends who cook and clean for me when I'm sick. Yet, when my mother was widowed, and then dying of cancer, I hardly ever visited her, never phoned, and never even spent part of my vacations with her. No one passed the house regularly except the mailman. She died of loneliness. I am haunted by my sins and have no peace. I'm an S.O.B. How could God ever forgive me?

ANSWER

Your guilt for the past is choking the life out of the present. Did you ever consider that you have been punished "**by**" your sins, not "**for**" them? When you chose not to visit your mother, you lost something by that decision. Not only did you miss a further closeness with your mother, but you also sacrificed your own growth. Choosing to not reach out, you were condemned to stay in, a decision that probably touched how you related to many in your life. That has been your punishment.

Yet, we are looking at this problem backwards, pessimistically seeing the glass half empty instead of half full. You must have learned from your mistakes if you have your friends dropping over to cook or care for you. Many people do not have such friends, and friendship is not simply due to the other person, it is also due to you!

Therefore, you need to stop punishing and start forgiving yourself. Forgiveness is based less on the forgiver being a nice person, and more on the ability of the sinner to change. God still loves you, not because God has to, but because you are still loveable. God sees beyond the mistakes that you have made in your life to the person underneath. God loves who you are, even if God may not be too crazy about what you do. If you are truly sorry, and wish to be a better person, that is all God wants.

God did not fall asleep on the day of your creation. You have the potential, the power, for change. Each day you get out of bed, you have another opportunity to grow more fully, whether you are 79 or 109. It makes no difference. As Yogi Berra once succinctly put it, "It ain't over till it's over."

So, while you have made some mistakes in the past, realize that we all have, and, as God has long since forgiven you, try to forgive yourself. Give equal airtime to your good points, and then try to love yourself so as to have more energy to love others. See each day as a challenge instead of a drudgery, and realize that while your body may be weak, who you are as a person is strong and still in formation.

KEY POINTS

- Stop punishing yourself today for mistakes yesterday. Your behavior was the punishment.
- As you always have the power to change and grow, forgive yourself, learn from your mistakes, and live a fuller life.

3. Caring for Your Parents

QUESTION: My father is 87 years old, quite infirm, and needs far more care than mom can give him. I have pleaded with them to have a home health aide come into the house, but both of them resist having a stranger in the house. Instead, they want me to do more and more for them. I try, but I am burning out, and my husband is angry at me for "neglecting" him. I feel so trapped. What can I do?

ANSWER

Today, as people tend to live longer lives, adult children end up having to care for their parents. This role reversal can be harder than many think. Many elderly refuse to allow "outsiders" into their home for fear of being robbed, and do not want to give up their house to go into assisted living or a nursing home. Instead, they want their children to "do it all", reminding their children of all that they did for them and now feeling entitled to a payback. But, the adult children often become burned out, and feel trapped between caring for their aging parents and caring for their spouse and children. What can they do?

If you are in this situation, my guess is that you know what to do, but are scared to do it. Perhaps you think that to be assertive with your mother or father is to be ungrateful and cruel, but actually, the opposite is true. Loving your parents is telling them the truth, and the truth is that you must both face your limitations.

Your mother and father must either allow a home-health aide and perhaps a visiting nurse into their home, or, if that is not feasible, agree to move to assisted living or a nursing home. Either way, you will still be involved. You will not only have to make these arrangements, but also help break in the aide so mom and dad see a friend instead of an intruder. And while many elderly see nursing homes as places to go to die, you will have to open their eyes to see the advantage of fuller, more round-the-clock services, not to mention many potential friends and activities to ease their sense of isolation.

As for yourself, this role reversal is certainly tough, being firm but kind with your mother and father seeming irreverent and disrespectful. But, while you will worry that you will one day appear on the cover of *People* magazine as the recipient of "The Worst Daughter of the Decade" award, you only have to reassure yourself that this will enable better care of not only them, but also yourself. Caring for mom and dad should not be at the price of not caring for you, your husband and your children. If it is, you will become increasingly bitter and resentful. So, while you might anger mom and dad at first, in the long run everyone will be better served.

KEY POINTS

- Setting realistic limits with your parents
  - o   is not being ungrateful or cruel, but
  - o   is allowing
    - better care for them,
    - while not burning yourself out, or neglecting your family.

OUR MAP: *Old Age*

PRINCIPLES and PROBLEMS
How our principles helped solve these problems.

__INSECURITY__: Instead of being stuck dwelling on past mistakes, try forgiving yourself and learning from them.

__POWER__: If retiring, your worth does not stop because your job did.

__SUCCESS__: You can still grow, your soul not slowing down because your body does.

FURTHER READING

- Delehanty, Hugh, and Elinor Ginzler, <u>Caring for Your Parents: The Complete AARP Guide</u>, New York, Sterling Publishing Company, 2005.
- Fries, James F., <u>Living Well: Taking Care of Yourself in the Middle and Later Years</u>, 4th Ed., Cambridge, MA, Da Capo Press, 2004.
- Snowdon, David, <u>Aging With Grace</u>, New York, Bantam Books, 2001.
- Taylor, Dan, <u>The Parent Care Conversation</u>, New York, Penguin Books, 2006.
- Thomas, William H., <u>What Are Old People For?</u>, Aeron, MA, VaderWyk & Burnham, 2004.

E. Illness

1. Coping with Illness

QUESTION: As if winter isn't dreadful enough, many have been hit by the flu this year. How does somebody cope with illness and keep their spirits up?

ANSWER

The mundane problem of catching a cold or the flu can certainly take the wind out of your sails. But take heart, coping with illness can help you to cope with life. If we can manage the tough times, then the rest of life should be "a piece of cake".

To begin with, coping with illness does not mean going *around* it, but rather growing *through* it. Facing your illness will help you develop skills with which to face your life, increasing your sense of happiness whether sick or not. Let me be more specific.

1. **FOCUS ON THE POSITIVES:** Your response to this caption is probably, "What positives?" Yes, if you have the flu, the negatives are all too apparent. You ache from head to toe, alternate from freezing to burning up, cannot stop coughing at night, and your nose is so red and irritated that you begin to resemble Rudolph the Red-Nosed Reindeer.

    But, instead of dwelling on what causes you pain, consider what brings you comfort: a warm cup of tea, Kleenex with aloe, curling up with a fuzzy blanket and a good book, renting a favorite video, and allowing your spouse and kids to fuss over you. Also, you become more aware of what you took for granted, such as taking a deep breath, sleeping through the night, and going through your day relatively pain free.

2. **AVOID NEGATIVE THINKING:** When sick with the flu or a bad cold which is responding all-too-slowly to your white blood cells and the doctor's medicine, you might get discouraged and say: "My life sucks", "I'm dying", "I wish I were dead", or "Why is God doing this to me". Try to calm down, and realize that your fear and frustration are being translated into unrealistic, overly negative thoughts. You will recover. Your life is not without meaning. And, God is not sitting on a cloud purposely deciding to ruin your day.

3. **REFRAME THE SITUATION**: Bad as your illness feels, it often can be a wake-up call, forcing you to take stock of yourself. Are you working too many hours? Not taking days off? Do your eating and exercising habits need a tad of reform?

    So, bad as it is, having the flu does give you time to rest, recoup your strength, and reflect on the meaning of your life. Instead of wallowing in how "crummy" you feel, why not reframe your temporary illness into more permanent corrections to your life?

4. **REFLECT ON LIFE**: Illness blatantly reminds us of our mortality, forcing us to reflect on the meaning of life. As we saw at the beginning of this book, it is not to live forever, for no matter how much health food you eat, or how much exercising you do, all of us will one day die. Hence, you are forced to ask the question of why you were born.

    One of the reasons that I wrote this book is that this question is so scary as to be dodged by most people, and so seemingly complex that pondering the answer seems beyond a simple person's grasp. However, as we have seen, it is relatively simple, namely, the purpose of your life is to decide who you wish to be by how you relate to others. Your choice being evidenced less by what you say and more by what you do. It is not a one-time choice, but a process of daily choices over the span of your life. The more you work on refining who you are, the more maturity and happiness are yours. When you die, the judgment of God is to accept your judgment, leaving you with the consequences of a lifetime of choices.

    Hence, being ill allows you to put things in perspective, and remember that happiness is defined less by how much you possess, and more by who you have become.

2. Cancer and Courage

QUESTION: I have a friend who is going through chemo. She has lost her hair, but not her courage. I have tried to understand how she holds it all together. Do you have any thoughts as to how people tough out cancer?

ANSWER

Eventually, colds and flu give way to more serious illnesses, and while the advice given above still applies, let me share some personal reflections of those who have combated cancer with courage.

Much of my learning has been from my own family. My father died of lung cancer, one of my older brothers died of lung and brain cancer, and my older sister died of liver cancer. My remaining brother and sister are in remission from cancer.

I rarely heard my family members complain. Instead, when I called or visited, their concern was amazingly how I was doing! I, like you, was struck by their courage and dignity. How did they cope? Here are just some of the things that they and other people over the years have helped me to see.

At first, the diagnosis of cancer hits like a bomb, destroying all sense of normalcy. While the immediate reaction is one of shock, MRIs and the tears of family quickly wash away any cloud of denial. Life then becomes consumed with facing fears like chemotherapy, especially with its concomitant nausea and loss of hair.

While the Pepsi Generation has for years told you that you would never grow old and die, your illness, even with a good prognosis, undeniably tells you of your mortality. If the flu makes you wonder about the meaning of your life, cancer glaringly shoves it in your face, and you begin to wonder if you really do believe in God and whether there is an afterlife.

If you do, your faith helps you eventually pass into a state of acceptance and peace, being scared of dying, but not of death. One person facing her death said to me, "It's sort of like going to a party where all your favorite people are waiting for you." The thought of Jesus waiting to see you with your mom and dad is very comforting, as is the thought that the last breath you take on your deathbed will be followed by the first breath that you take in heaven.

But what about today? Many people see through their illness not only to the next life, but also to this one. The possible loss of life makes them aware of the gift of each day. Their comment is why waste time and energy being bitter or dwelling on what is bad. Instead, why not make the best of a bad situation, and turn it into something good.

Research tells us that giving in or focusing too much on our loss compromises our immunity, brings down our resistance. Concentrating on what you have instead of what you have lost gives you mental ammunition to use in your physical fight. One person, who died on the same day that I spoke to him, noted, "I have so much that to bitch would be a sin." On his final day, he helped me live all my future days. Unable to lift his head, he forever lifted my spirit. I hope my words lift yours.

KEY POINTS

- <u>Afterlife</u>: Faith brings peace, no longer fearing death even if still fearing the process of dying.
- <u>This Life</u>:
  - o The risk of no more tomorrows makes us aware of the gift of today.
  - o Concentrate on what health you have instead of what you have lost.
  - o Concentrate on the positives; deal with the negatives, but do not dwell on them.

3. Waiting Room Agonies

QUESTION: My wife is seriously ill, and enduring a crammed waiting room for hours seems to add insult to injury. I get so impatient and grumpy, complaining to my wife when I should be a better support for her. How can I turn this around?

ANSWER

We have looked at how to cope if you are ill. But, what if you are the spouse of the person who is ill? How can you cope better?

As I like concrete advice, picture the common situation of you in a waiting room. Having the appointment is often nerve-racking enough, for either your spouse is having one more test or procedure, nervously awaiting the results of those tests, or having another check-up that confirms how sick she is without offering any real relief.

But, then you enter a waiting room that is standing room only, overly warm because of all that body heat. You luck out and get to sit next to the person who flunked "Hygiene 101" in high school. You look at many patients who stare ahead vacantly and their spouses who bury their fears by burying their heads in a book or magazine, and the optimism to which you cling seems more tenuous than ever. Then, you reflect on the reality of a long wait until your wife is called, and then waiting for her to reemerge. Indeed, waiting room agonies "add insult to injury".

While we could write another article on why some physicians "double book" patients, your question is how to cope with the reality before you. Here are a few simple ideas, none of which are perfect, but all of which will help.

ATTITUDE: The same advice that applies to your spouse who is ill applies to you. While there is no denying the negatives, why dwell on them? Even if your spouse was dying, endlessly going over the gloomy details will not help anyone. Instead, what are the genuine positives of the moment? At first, you cannot see them, but then there they are, right under your nose. Perhaps it is a cold soda or hot coffee while you are waiting, time to talk with your spouse or quietly reflect on the meaning of your life, the color and smell of flowers in the room, a beautiful picture on the wall, a good article to read, and people with whom to visit.

SERVICE: The waiting room is ironically a self-imposed support group. Everyone has a similar problem, but everyone handles it differently. You can learn from them, or teach a new way of coping that brought you relief. Also, should someone need a cup of water or the channel on the TV changed, helping them with such a simple need will awaken in you a depth of compassion and growth.

HUMOR: Lightening a heavy mood by a witty comment or joke can sometimes make a day of mounting unpleasantries more tolerable. I remember once while waiting with my wife to take a test that required fasting, sitting with other patients also feeling famished due to having to fast, a delivery person came into the office with a large tray of sandwiches for the doctors and their staff. Everyone's eyes were riveted on the sandwiches that were essentially forbidden fruit, and I quipped, "Talk about torture". Everyone burst out laughing, and I suggested that we all go out for pancakes and bacon after the tests. The relief in the room was almost palpable, and the sense of comradeship made everyone feel more connected and less alone.

Also, when illness strikes in a family, try to watch more comedies and less "gut-wrenching" dramas on TV, as coping with what is on your plate is enough to face. This applies to a waiting room just as much as it does to your own family room.

DEEP BREATHING: Try taking longer breathes than normal, inhaling from your stomach, and giving your active mind a rest by focusing upon any object across the room. Let distracting thoughts come and go instead of latching onto to them, and notice that in five minutes your stress will slowly decrease.

PRAYER: And finally, you can combine deep breathing with meditation, reflecting on how Christ endured the agony in the garden, how much God loves you, or what it means for God to be your Father.

OUR MAP: *Illness*

PRINCIPLES and PROBLEMS
How our principles helped solve these problems.

<u>POWER</u>: You are more than your illness, and so can grow through it.

<u>SUCCESS</u>: Being temporarily unable to **do**, reflect upon who you **are** still able to become.

FURTHER READING

- Allen, Jennifer, <u>I Can Survive</u>, New York, McGraw Hill, 2007.
- Bouvard, Marguerite Guzman, <u>Healing A Life with Chronic Illness</u>, London, University Press of New England, 2007.
- Grinyer, Anne, <u>Young People Living with Cancer</u>, New York, McGraw Hill, 2007.

F. Death

1. Facing Death

QUESTION: I have a close friend who is dying. What must he be feeling and how can I help?

QUESTION: I recently was told that my illness is "terminal", a rather stiff way of telling me that I am dying. Ever since that day, I have felt overwhelmed with what seems like a tidal wave of feelings. Sometimes, I think that I am losing my mind. Am I?

ANSWER

We now move from a person who is ill to one who is dying. This can be the scariest time of your life, but it is also one where you can feel empowered, your growth touching many deeply and forever. As did Kubler-Ross, I see discernable steps in the process of facing death.

<u>DENIAL</u>: The shock of the diagnosis of a terminal illness initially hits like a sledgehammer, taking your breath away as your eyes fill with tears. However, once home amidst your usual surroundings, and not yet aware of dramatically unusual symptoms, the shock can fade quickly and seem almost unreal.

It is reasonable for you to need time to be able to swallow what you have just been told, as well as denial being the mind's protection from being overwhelmed. However, failure to keep appointments or begin treatment may require those who care to lovingly, but firmly, confront you with the reality of your situation.

Another form of denial can be hoping for a miracle. Can a cure occur? Yes, but not often. And remember, the meaning of life is not to live forever. Occasionally, our belief in the wonders of modern medicine or a miracle from God can not only cloud the reality of death, but also condemn the dying to a miserable one. A person can cling to the hope that they will magically be returned to health, and thus be unwilling to accept what is happening to them and prepare not only themselves but also their family for death.

<u>ANGER</u>: But soon your illness aggressively confronts you with the painful reality of invasive symptoms. No matter how old you are, you feel robbed of normalcy, and, being only able to slow this agonizing journey, you rail against what

seems unfair and capricious. Not being able to scream at your illness, you strike out at your spouse, family, doctor and God, all of whom will hopefully stay calm and listen empathetically, redirecting your energies to fight your illness and face the meaning of your life.

BARGAINING: Mixed in with anger at others can be anger at self, cruelly torturing yourself with wondering "what if" you did this or that to have avoided the quandary in which you now feel trapped. Again, others help you to face the inevitable consequences of being human, that life on earth does not last forever no matter how many "T's" you cross or "I's" you dot, but is instead a path to a life hereafter.

Some people, much like Job, wonder if they are being punished in the present for past sins. But, God is not vindictive. The punishment for selfish behavior is to BE selfish, God's judgment, having given you free will, is to accept your judgment. But, remember, your life is most probably more good than bad, and even if it was not, you can change right up until you die, God forever offering you forgiveness and another chance.

DEPRESSION: As the disease process inexorably and insidiously deepens, with pain increasing and quality of life decreasing, trips to the doctor or hospital seem ever so futile, and the inevitability of what is approaching depresses you.

Incredibly, when you most need people, many shy away from you, scared to face their own mortality, and soothing their hidden guilt by dismissing you with "I'll be praying for you", their prayers ringing hollow without being backed up by the actions of calling, visiting or feeding you.

Even those who do visit may nervously give false reassurances that "it'll be OK", when you know that is just not true. You then feel increasingly alone, and your depression worsens.

Friends need to let you air your feelings, and give you honest feedback, helping you prepare for death. And, as strange as this sounds, you need to focus more on the good than the bad. The negatives are all-too-evident, being rudely shoved "right in your face". But, to dwell on them gets you nowhere. Instead, focus on what is genuinely good in your life, such as the love of your family and God, the warmth of the sun on your face or coffee on your palate, the softness of a robe, clean sheets on your bed, and flowers from a friend—these are real, but often missed in our hectic world. Now you have time to notice the small things, and that will make a large difference.

ACCEPTANCE: Gradually, you are drawn to face your death because it is constantly looming before you, and honest talks with God, your pastor, and your spouse move you from seeing death as an end to seeing that it is a transition to a new beginning. Looking back at your life helps you to see the maturation of your soul; your chosen ability to connect with and love others being a treasure that death cannot touch. You then become not scared of death, but only of the process of dying, realizing that the last breath you take on earth will be followed by the first breath you take in heaven, enabling you to let go of one life to embrace another.

2. What *NOT* to Say

*QUESTION: My wife died recently, and I was struck by how many dumb comments were made to me, like "It's God's Will." Could you write an article to help people know what **not** to say when bad times hit?*

ANSWER

When a person dies, people are not sure what to say, and often rely on trite phrases that they hope will plug the hole of **their** anxiety. As the focus needs to be on the person whom they are trying to comfort rather than themselves, they hurt instead of help, and so need to learn what **not** to say. Here are a few examples of what I mean.

<u>It's God's Will</u>: Does it make sense that a God who loves you would want to hurt you? While the purpose of life is not to live forever, God creating a finite and temporal world that eventually ends in death, that does not mean that a conniving God plays with our lives like Zeus atop Mount Olympus, throwing troubles in our way to see what we shall do. Instead of giving a theology lesson, why not ask if the person would be comforted to have their priest, minister, or rabbi visit them?

<u>Death was a Blessing</u>: To whom? If you mean that the person died quickly instead of enduring a slow, lingering death, while that may be true, it does not remove the fact that a parent or spouse is now dead. Instead of trying to make something bad good, why not tell your friend how sad you are for them?

<u>I know how you feel</u>: Really? Even if you ooze of empathy, you do not really know how anybody else feels. Why not simply ask them how *they* are feeling, and then just listen. This is about them, not you.

<u>You're Young and Can Remarry</u>: Maybe so, but that does not remove the present pain, and unwittingly implies that the other person can be replaced. To remarry is to begin with a new person, not to erase the old one from memory.

<u>Call me if I can help</u>: But will they? Have you thought that maybe the other person does not want to impose on you? Instead of waiting for a call, why not call yourself, offering some specific help, like cooking a meal, washing laundry, mowing their lawn, walking their dog, et cetera.

I'll be praying for you: On the surface, this sounds good, but often is a way of pushing the other away with pious platitudes, perhaps due to your own fear of facing your mortality. Faith without charity is empty, so why not offer some concrete help like I just mentioned, or call to come back and pray **with** the other person, not just *for* them.

A final comment is that when I was a young priest, I worried about what to say when visiting someone who was ill or dying, hoping to come up with just the right thought or prayer. But age has taught me that my caring presence was more important than any pearls of wisdom. So, do not sell short the value of just being there for someone, offering not a quick duty visit, but one that shows how much you really care.

3. Death of Your Spouse

QUESTION: My husband just died. I feel like my life is over. I am so alone, and know that I shall never find anyone to love again. People nicely tell me that I have to "get it together". What the heck does that mean? I feel so lost. Can you help?

ANSWER

Facing the death of a spouse is followed immediately by trying to cope with suddenly being alone. Caring for a dying spouse consumes your every waking moment. When your spouse dies, you go from feeling exhausted and overwhelmed by all that must be done to being alone while trying to cope with conflicting feelings and a painful adjustment to a new life.

Having lost my wife after a liver transplant, after literally years of fighting to hold onto life, I write not only as someone who has helped others cope, but also as someone who was helped to cope. Here are some of the problems that you might encounter, and some solutions that you might find helpful.

1. **Problems to Understand**:

   a. *Fear*: Having had a life that was shared, you probably will have fears of being alone, not just now, but forever. You may aimlessly wander around your house calling out your spouse's name and wondering where he or she is, continually asking yourself "what am I going to do without you?"

      Be reassured that your genuine strength to cope is real, just having dealt with your spouse's terminal illness being one powerful example. Hence, you will cope. But be patient. Mourning is not on a timer. And when friends and family want to visit or invite you to dinner, let them. My only hope being that they are present, not just at first, but over the next year.

   b. *Anger*: Ironically, you may also experience anger at your spouse, whom you may feel left you with unpaid bills, should have taken better care of himself, forced you to raise the kids alone, to return to school for training for a job, or just to get a job. While you will know these angry thoughts are irrational, let yourself get them off your chest, the role of friends being to listen with empathy and let you vent.

   c. *Guilt*: If your marriage was rocky, you may punish yourself with regrets at not having been more loving and attentive, less selfish and demanding, and less critical and judgmental. I encourage you, as would your spouse, to forgive yourself, realizing that your behavior hurt you as well as your spouse, that you are capable of much better behavior, and that this wake-up call is a final gift from your spouse.

d.   *Awkwardness*: As your friends are most likely married, going to functions may make you feel like the fifth wheel on a wagon, perhaps even making you envious of them. Realize that your friends are adjusting to you being alone just as are you, and it will be important that they do not just invite you, but consciously include you in conversations, making you feel more comfortable.

e.   *Embarrassment of Crying in Public*: A song on the radio, a fragrance reminiscent of your husband's after shave, birthdays, anniversaries, and holidays all may cause you to unexpectedly cry. You are not losing it. While mourning occurs largely in the weeks after someone dies, it also continues for months to come. After all, the goal is not to forget your spouse, but rather to process your loss.

2.   **Solutions to Suggest**:

a.   *Time to heal*: As I noted above, give yourself time to heal instead of feeling "crazy" because of a continuing mélange of feelings after six to eight weeks.

b.   *No Major Decisions in First Year*: You may want to sell your house, change jobs, relocate, or make some other major decision in the first year. My advice, "What's the rush?"

c.   *Finding a New Social Life and New Friends*: As old friends come with old memories and uncomfortable social events, you may want to find new friends. I do not mean to replace old friends, but rather to complement them. Some of your friends may be a bit jealous, but my guess is that most will be very understanding.

d.   *Turning Loneliness into Solitude*: Loneliness is not necessarily a dirty word. Facing one's inner demons, becoming more comfortable with one's self, learning yoga, meditation and relaxation techniques may turn a feared enemy into a new friend.

e.   *Adopt a Pet*: Of course, loneliness has an undeniable negative side. Adopting a pet can ease the pain. Walking in the front door to find a dog practically exploding with joy to see you, and then following you from room to room is a wonderful feeling and good companionship.

f.   *Ask for Help*: Talk with your rabbi, minister or priest not only for advice, but also for the support the congregation can provide.

g.   *Keep a Journal*: You may find comfort and some inner control by keeping a journal of your thoughts and feelings, helping you to not dwell on the negative or ignore the positive.

h.   *TLC*: Force yourself to eat well and exercise (walking/gardening is fine), while avoiding too much caffeine, and not using drugs or alcohol to cope.

i.   *Remarry?* I left the most difficult one for last.

  While you will need time to heal before thinking of remarrying, you will also need to realize that doing so is not an insult to your deceased spouse. Your vow to love one another on your wedding day ended with the words, "until we are parted by death". You have lovingly and honorably fulfilled your promise. If you believe in heaven, you know that your spouse is perfectly happy. Why would they not want you to be happy?

  Of course, people think that when they die, how will they explain to the spouse who died that they remarried? And, who will they be married to in heaven? Well, Jesus himself had to wrestle with that question (Luke 20: 27-38), being posed the question of a woman who had seven husbands. The answer is that there is no marriage in heaven.

  While this may shock you, it does not imply that you will not see your spouse who has died, nor that you will not be together with them. But what it does say is that the purpose of marriage on earth is to help you grow, the creative interaction between husband and wife helping each to polish the diamond that is their personality. Death is the end of growth.

  In heaven, you will be as you have chosen to be, now for all eternity. Hence, the interaction between a husband and wife will not be to grow, but simply to enjoy the state of bliss that goes on forever. Having been married to two people during your one life will simply mean that you will all be happy together; no jealousy, just joy.

  So, after you have sufficiently mourned, and when you determine that you are ready, why not reach for the happiness that married life brings you? God and your deceased spouse love you and would want you to be as happy as humanly possible.

4. Till Death Us Do Part

In addition to the advice just given, I thought that you might also like me to share a profound insight that I experienced during the death of my wife, Nicolina ("Nicki"). She died on October 8, 2004. The cause of death was her body rejecting the liver that was transplanted into her on July 14, 2001. The experience that I am describing happened while facing her impending death once she was moved into a hospice program on October 3, 2004.

When we marry, we promise to be faithful until we are parted by death. Today, I find many who think of that as a time to be feared, as a bitter pill to be swallowed, or as an obligation owed in repayment for all the good and healthy years. Still others, seeing decreasing health in a spouse, contemplate divorce to escape mixing such pain and sadness with the previous years of pleasure and happiness.

Of course, no one wants his or her spouse to die. I worked with every fiber of my being to return my wife to health, affording her every measure of care possible. But, when I had to travel through suffering to death with her, I discovered a new and deeper level of love. Doctors focus solely on preserving life, but patients often know when death is coming. My wife told me that she was dying a month before she died. I was slower to accept that reality, but when she entered a hospice program, invasive procedures stopped and facing death together entered a very intensive phase.

Entering the room where you will die is a somber moment. Imagine as they wheel you into a hospital room what it must be like to realize that the only way you will be leaving this room is after you die.

When I went to go home at the end of that day, my wife was understandably upset, and I decided to spend the night in the room with her. The nurses wanted me to stay in a home nearby the hospital, but I refused. Then they said that they would compromise and allow me to sleep in a room at the end of the hallway where doctors slept, but I again refused, saying that I was not going to leave my wife alone. Eventually, they conceded and gave me what amounted to a cot that I positioned so that we could look directly at each other's face.

Nicki had just come off of another two-week period on a respirator and so could barely speak above a whisper, her throat having being affected by the tubing. Not wanting her to try and speak, but wanting to communicate, I pointed to my eye, then my heart, and then her, conveying "I love you", and she, unable to lift her arms, mouthed the same back to me. She looked inquisitively at me at one point, and when I said that I was crying, her eyes reached across the room to comfort me. We then stared at each other for about three hours, never speaking a word, our eyes riveted on each other, giving the sense that there was no distance between us. It was as if we were hugging each other with our eyes. This continued until she fell asleep due to occasional morphine injections to hold her pain at bay. I have never felt anything that powerful before in my life!

Marriage ceremonies talk about the two becoming one. That night we were one. Nicki died five nights later. She was in and out of consciousness, and we never again had the clarity of that one night, but it was an experience that has sustained me through her death and into my life without her.

My words to you feel clumsy and awkward, unable to convey the power of the love felt. My only wish is to ease your fear of walking towards death with your spouse. Amidst the inescapable pain, there will also be the culmination of your love in ultimate intimacy. You will experience the joy of being one. Those who allow their fear to make them run from death will lose one of the purest gifts of life, let alone be haunted with the memory of not being there when they were most needed.

5. Kids and Death

QUESTION: How do you explain death to a child? I have tried to shelter my 7-year old son from all that is bad, but when my father who is terminally ill and whom he loves dies, what do I do? Do I take him to the wake or funeral, or not at all?

ANSWER

How do you explain death to a child? Parents try to shelter their children from all that is bad, but when a parent or grandparent becomes terminally ill and dies, what can you as a parent do?

<u>**HELP HIM MOURN**</u>: I understand how you feel. You spend every waking hour trying to protect your son or daughter from anything that could hurt them. But, death is part of life, and when their grandparents regrettably die, mourning is a process that they will go through with or without you. So, helping them on this journey will not only comfort them, but also build an ever-closer bond with you.

<u>**HOW KIDS SEE DEATH**</u>: How children experience death varies according to their age.

- *Children under age 5* perceive death as a temporary, reversible state in which the person is still alive but motionless, essentially *asleep* for a long time.
- *Children between ages 5-9*, like your son, view death as a fearful state in which the person is *separated from his or her family*. It is seen as an unlucky event for some instead of a certainty for all. Finally, for
- *Children over 9*, there emerges an adult view of death as *the end of life*.

<u>**HOW TO SPEAK TO YOUR CHILD**</u>: As the experience of the child varies, so too does the explanation. The older the child, the more developed the explanation. If your child has known and loved their grandparents, he or she will want to talk about what has happened. But even then, remember that a child does not have the emotional strength to tolerate the painful effects of prolonged grieving like an adult. So, pick your moments.

Obviously, the day you tell your child that your father or mother has died, as well as the day of the wake and the funeral, will prompt numerous questions. But, realize that places or objects that remind your child of your father or mother, or a movie dealing with the death of a person or pet will also bring the subject right back into focus. Don't panic; just take time for a heart-to-heart chat.

RELIGION: Religion can be very helpful, as it points to the connection between this life and the next. Explaining to a child that their grandparent, aunt or uncle is with God and very happy can be very comforting and give meaning to the painful separation that they are feeling. This is not a myth to comfort the weak, but a belief about the purpose of life ... one that will comfort you, as well as your child.

WAKE OR FUNERAL? Should your child go to the wake or funeral? Some have said that the wake, where the child can see the body, makes death easier to understand than looking at a closed coffin in the aisle of a church. But, both events give your child, as they do you, the opportunity to cry, ask questions, be comforted, and say goodbye. However, remember that going to a wake or funeral can be very confusing, and must be accompanied by a talk where you take your time, try to give an age-appropriate explanation, and thoughtfully answer whatever questions your child may ask.

A FINAL THOUGHT: I know that talking about the death of your father or mother with your child will be one of the hardest things that you will ever have to do, but how fortunate that he or she will have you there to guide them. Your love and sensitivity will heal their wound, mature your soul, and forever be remembered as a tender moment between the two of you.

6. Youth Suicide

QUESTION: I was surprised to find out that the number of suicides among children has increased in recent years. Why is that? And, if a child commits suicide, how could I help?

ANSWER

A shocking reality is that the number of suicides among children has increased, not only for adolescents as some might expect, but also for pre-adolescents, which many find shocking. Why is that and how can you help?

1. **WHY**: There is no one reason. The pressure of school performance, glamorizing suicide in the media, a child's changing perception of death, personal or family emotional difficulties, drug abuse, and biochemical changes in the child are but a few reasons. But in discussing reasons, seek to understand, not blame. And, try to face rather than explain away what is so upsetting.

2. **COMMON REACTIONS & HOW TO HELP**: You can help children cope with the suicide of a classmate by acknowledging how much they hurt, encouraging them to express their feelings, and letting them know what to expect as they grieve. Remember that it is a process, and so strong feelings can be triggered not only by television coverage of the suicide days after the loss, but also by a movie months later about death or suicide. Some specific reactions and how you can help are:

   a. *Denial*: Communicate facts in a clear and concise way. Realize that the younger the child, the more gradually they will be able to mourn their loss. So, be patient and available; do not push.

   b. *Anger*: Allow kids to express it, but avoid scapegoating parents or society.

   c. *Guilt*: Reassure kids that they did not cause the death, and give permission to enjoy life amidst their grief.

   d. *Sadness*: Listen with empathy, encourage discussion, and validate feelings. What might assist children to express their feelings is artwork if they are young and writing in journals if they are older.

e. *Shame*: Reassure kids that crying and talking about feelings is healthy and a sign of strength. A support group of peers will help, as will adults (especially men) being vulnerable in sharing their own feelings.

3. **COMMUNITY RESOURCES**: You are not alone. Help your child cope with the death of a friend by using your school, church, synagogue, and local counseling service. Schools, for example, often have organized plans and crisis response teams, which help children express their feelings in a controlled and organized manner, identify and work with the families of children thought to be at-risk, and help faculty through their own process of grieving.

4. **AT-RISK CHILDREN**: Among children who deserve special attention after a suicide are close friends or "enemies" of the deceased, those who have experienced recent losses (moved to a new home away from family and friends), those fascinated with death and suicide, and children who have exhibited problem behaviors (depression, drug abuse, or suicide attempts of their own). Parents should also be watchful should there be an increase in physical ailments and/or a decrease in academic performance.

OUR MAP: *Death*

PRINCIPLES and PROBLEMS
How our principles helped solve these problems.

__INSECURITY__: The roller coaster of feelings is normal. You are not "losing it", just dealing with it.

__POWER__: People's avoidance of you is really avoidance of facing death.

__SUCCESS__: Even though you are at your weakest physically, you are ironically at your strongest psychologically to teach others what really matters, as death makes us reflect upon the meaning of life.

FURTHER READING

- Bermar, Alan L., David A. Jobes, and Morton M. Silverman, <u>Adolescent Suicides: Assessment and Intervention</u>, Washington, DC, American Psychological Association, 2005.

- Capossela, Cappy and Sheila Warnock, <u>Share the Care: How to Organize A Group to Care for Someone Who is Seriously Ill</u>, New York, Simon & Schuster, 1995.

- Kubler-Ross, Elisabeth, <u>On Death and Dying</u>, New York, Scribner, 1969.

- Nuland, Sherwin B., <u>How to Die: Reflections on Life's Final Chapter</u>, New York, Vintage Books, 1993.

- Rando, Therese A., <u>How to Go on Living When Someone You Love Dies</u>, New York, Bantam Books, 1988.

- Shaw, Eva, <u>What to do When a Loved One Dies: A Practical and Compassionate Guide to Dealing with the Death in Life's Terms</u>, Irvine, CA, Dickens Press, 1994.

- Underwood, Maureen M., and Karen Dunne-Maxim, <u>Managing Sudden Traumatic Loss in the Schools</u>, Piscataway, NJ, University Behavioral HealthCare, 1997.

G. The Holidays

1. The Holiday Blues

QUESTION: *I'm dreading the holidays. Every year at this time, I get a bad case of "the blues", and can't seem to shake them. My family gets frustrated with me, and I just don't understand why I'm down when everybody else is up. What can I do to cope better?*

ANSWER

Why is it that some people dread the holidays, often getting a bad case of "the blues"? To understand why many people get depressed during what most people picture as the happiest time of the year, we must look at what was and what might have been.

1. **WHAT WAS**: Imagine someone whose parents or spouse has recently died. Their first Christmas alone finds their minds irresistibly drawn back to past holidays filled with laughter and joy, all the more intensifying their feelings of loss. While this phenomenon is normal, and while one adjusts to death with time, nonetheless, it is important to note that some remnant of this feeling will remain, the holidays forever having a twinge of pain amidst a season of cheer.

2. **WHAT MIGHT HAVE BEEN**: Far more difficult is the problem of what might have been. Imagine now someone who has been recently divorced. The holidays, a time when families are together with children "nestled in their beds" finds this person often bitterly separated from their spouse and grudgingly shuffling their children back and forth hoping to foster some semblance of family. Knowing it could be different, this person agonizes over what might have been if only certain mistakes had not been made, usually in their mind by the other person.

3. **WHAT WAS BAD**: Now think of someone whose past is anything but happy, perhaps having lived at odds with their parents, feeling that their parents never really cared. Imagine the pain of an adult child of an alcoholic or an adult survivor of incest. Watching numerous saccharine and ubiquitous Christmas specials on television depicting unrealistically happy

families sitting arm in arm together in front of "the old Yule log" may be torture, producing feelings of jealousy, sadness, and intense anger.

4. **WHAT CAN HELP?**

    a. ***What Was Good***: We need to cherish our memories, realizing that our loved ones would not want us to endlessly suffer. They would want us to go on, reassuring us that to enjoy today is not to be disrespectful to yesterday.

    b. ***What Might Have Been***: While it is important to reflect on a past divorce to learn from our mistakes, it is not healthy to dwell on them. Instead of being stuck on what was lost in the past, it seems best to free ourselves to see what we have in the present.

    c. ***What Was Bad***: Dealing with emotional or physical abuse from childhood is far more difficult, probably requiring therapy, expressing anger assertively when possible, and, ultimately, forgiveness.

    d. ***Perfect Happiness***: Some of what underlies the holiday blues is an innate desire to be perfectly happy. Unfortunately, this is an impossible task, for perfect happiness can only be attained through union with a perfect being, namely, God. Our earthly life, being limited, is, therefore, open to suffering. We all need to reflect upon the true meaning of Christmas and of life, realizing that Christ was born in a manger and died on a cross, but brought us eternal salvation. That Christmas present will not fade or tarnish, its value being so wonderful as to bring a smile to our face, and, hopefully, us to church to give thanks.

2. Thanksgiving

Thanks for What?

QUESTION: Forgive me for being a cynic, but what is Thanksgiving really all about? We seem to always be under the threat of terrorism. My wife and I have been arguing more than usual. And if that was not enough, I just got a horrible case of the flu. Now, you clergy are telling me to celebrate Thanksgiving by thanking God for all he has done for me. Thanks for what?

ANSWER

Certainly, we all have a lot on our plates, but getting lost in a negative forest of cynicism is not going to help. Here are a few thoughts.

1. **FOCUS ON THE POSITIVES**: All too often the intrusive, in-your-face negatives of life cloud our vision. While we should face problems squarely, there is little to be gained by dwelling on them. Instead, we need to not magnify the negatives, but see them in the light of countless positives that we all too often take for granted. Below are but a few.

2. **WHAT POSITIVES?**
   a. *Health*: OK, you have the flu. But, you will recover. Aching and coughing will be replaced with ease of movement and the ability to take a deep breath. Even in the midst of the flu, you will be able to read a book, watch TV, take a nap, and warm yourself with a hot cup of tea and a fuzzy blanket.
   b. *A Renewed Sense of Caring*: While the terrorists challenged our ability to feel safe, our government has taken steps to protect us when we are on a plane or at work. And, born from the hatred of the terrorists has been a reawakened sense of love for each other, changing us from a "ME" to a "WE" society where heroes big and small emerge to challenge the notion that no one really cares.
   c. *Spouse*: While you would like to punch a terrorist in the nose, you cannot. Hence, we tend to displace our frustration and anger onto those closest to us. Instead, talk out your feelings instead of biting the hand that feeds you. Realize how lucky you are to have someone who loves

you, and while he or she may have a few weaknesses, their strengths are far greater, and, after all, you are no Prince either.

d.   ***Senses***: How fortunate you are to be able to see a sunset, listen to a concert, smell flowers, taste a turkey dinner, and feel the warmth of a hot shower.

e.   ***Intellect***: Imagine not being able to go to school, read a magazine, talk with a friend, or creatively solve an annoying problem.

f.   ***Will***: You can love and be loved, the caring of spouse, kids and friends making up for an army of bad breaks.

g.   ***God***: You are so loved by God that he was born in a manger instead of a palace, grew up as a carpenter in Nazareth instead of as a Prince in Jerusalem, and died naked on a cross for your sins instead of being surrounded by his family and friends at his bedside.

h.   ***Salvation***: The result of God's love is your salvation. We would jump for joy if a doctor could extend our lives by 10 years. How about eternity!

So, there is plenty for which to give thanks. Dust off your bifocals, kiss your spouse, bend your knee in church, and see the treasures that surround you every day of your life, even in the midst of all our troubles.

3. Christmas

a. Surviving Christmas

QUESTION: I hate Christmas. It's just pressure, pressure, pressure! I'm always exhausted when it's over, feeling like I have run some kind of endurance race. Am I weird? Is my complaint common? Got any ideas of what I could do?

ANSWER

Well, having reconnected with the true meaning of Thanksgiving, we sail on to Christmas only to discover that many view it as weeks of exhausting pressure, running through a gauntlet of long lines at stores, and relatives that plop themselves down on your couch and do not help prepare for or clean up dinner.

If this sounds like you, the pressure cooker in which you find yourself during the holiday season is strangely created by you! You have unwittingly given others the power to determine your worth, instead of calmly deciding what it is that you can and cannot do. You cannot please all the people all the time, no matter how much money you spend on gifts or how lavish a party you throw. So, pull the plug on the pressure by bravely deciding what you **want** to do instead of what you feel that you **have** to do. Remember, this involves one of the principles underlying your search for happiness, namely, taking back the power to determine your own worth rather than giving that power to the couch potatoes.

Let's look at four areas of stress to make my point clear.

1. **SHOPPING**:
    - Realize that there is no "perfect present", and that your goal is to demonstrate love, not to outdo previous years with oohs and ahs.
    - Try not to overspend in an effort to overcompensate for too much quantity of time at work and too little quality time at home. Instead, reinvest yourself in your family.
    - And, if you really want to go for the brass ring of mall maturity, be courteous to the discourteous, and try not to have a short temper while waiting in a long line.

2. **FAMILY**:

- Put the needs of your spouse and children before the pressures of family and friends. It's OK to tell your mother that you are celebrating Christmas in your own home, and to visit fewer relatives so as to do so out of love rather than duty.

- If you are short on money, then cut or eliminate your long list of people designated for Christmas cards, and consider giving one gift instead of many to your spouse and children.

- Therefore, a good rule of thumb to adopt is to consider doing less so as to enjoy the holidays more.

3. **CHURCH**: To take the stress out of Christmas, try putting Christ back into it. Instead of threatening your spouse and children with bodily harm if they do not accompany you to church, consider reminding them of the real meaning of Christmas. I am not talking about a stern and "boring" lecture that will turn everyone off, but rather a discussion about the meaning of love. How much God must love us to have allowed his Son to be born in a manger instead of a palace, wrapped in swaddling clothes instead of silk, living in a town so obscure that it is not even mentioned in the Old Testament, and then being willing to die for us on a cross. Therefore, we go to church not out of duty with a gun to our head, but out of love and a desire to rediscover the meaning of our lives.

4. **TV SPECIALS**: If you came from an abusive family, or if your parents or spouse have died, or if you have been through a divorce, the endless onslaught of maudlin TV specials, depicting happy "normal" families might make you think that your family is anything but normal. And yet, what we are shown is an ideal towards which we all strive, the attainment of which is never fully within our grasp. We should not be discouraged by this image, just patient and persistent in our journey towards it. Remember another one of our principles, all people feel insecure, including you, me and the Pope.

b. Priceless Presents

QUESTION: *Christmas makes me feel like such a loser. All anyone ever thinks about is how many presents they're getting and how much they cost. I'm just an ordinary guy who doesn't have much to give his wife and kids. I come out of this season of greed just thinking that I just don't measure up. Can you help me?*

ANSWER

Like millions of others, this poor guy had fallen into the materialistic trap of thinking that his value as a person was based upon how much he made and spent. Does that sound at all like you? If so, consider that while all of us will do our best to buy gifts for our family, all you really need to do is to try to think of some meaningful and priceless presents that you can give to your spouse and children that will not fade, rust, or end up in the back of the closet. Consider giving YOU as a gift, offering your family your:

1.   **TIME:** There is only so much of you to go around. Rethink who you donate you to, perhaps cutting back here or there so as to be able to take your spouse out for a walk and a talk, to show up at your daughter's school play, or just stay at home, rent a video, and enjoy each other's company.

2.   **EMPATHY:** Instead of getting defensive when your spouse or child tells you their angry or hurt feelings, work hard to listen intently to how they are feeling, summarizing what they said and asking if you got it right. Whether it be your spouse arguing for a new kitchen table or your teenage son for a later curfew, put yourself in their shoes before trying to give your knee-jerk reaction. Whether you end up buying the table or bending on the curfew, your spouse and son will know that you care enough to listen.

3.   **PATIENCE:** Waiting without blowing your top while your preschool daughter ties her shoes before you take her to daycare helps her to develop autonomy and you to develop tolerance for life's ups and downs. Your lower blood pressure will mean fewer arguments at home, less stress on the job, and more happiness for you.

4.   **SMILE:** Instead of being grumpy, cynical, and an old grouch, try forcing yourself to smile a little bit each day. Amazingly, you will find that it

is somewhat contagious, your spouse and children exchanging their sad frowns for a happy face, and you yourself reframing what you thought was "a disastrous problem" into "a challenging opportunity". Gradually, you will be turning your family into optimists and problem solvers, for which all of us will thank you.

So, my advice is that you stop worrying about what you cannot buy, and start thinking about how you impact on your family, more so than any teacher, peer, movie, or book. You have the ability to give them the priceless gift of yourself, which you will not find at *Macy's* or *Toys R' Us,* or even at the *North Pole,* just under your own nose.

4. New Year's Resolutions

QUESTION: *What's the use in making New Year's Resolutions? I make them on the 1*st *and break them on the 2*nd*!*

ANSWER

When I got this letter in the mail, my first response was to not be so hard on himself, noting that many make and break them on the 1st!!! But, does that mean that you should never make a New Year's Resolution? Of course not.

Remember, happiness is a process, not a product. It is not something you buy on sale at *Macy's*, but something that you work on each day of your life. The real intent is to think of New Year's as a wake-up call to the goal of a "New You". Actually, it is a "Better You", building upon past efforts and present strengths, rather than starting from scratch and inventing a new person.

While we try not to see this process as a daily drudgery, we admittedly get stuck walking down the path of life. So, we need to rekindle the fire, helping ourselves get back on track. To do this, we use various points in our year to check on how we are doing and to restart our engines. Some of us use Advent or Lent, Rosh Hashanah or Yom Kippur, birthdays or anniversaries, and still others use New Year's Day.

Therefore, New Year's resolutions are a good idea. So, why not take this New Year's as an opportunity to take stock of who you are, and of what issues you would like to gradually work.

- **Do you have a temper?** Then try to express your anger calmly and with sensitivity, instead of holding it in until you explode or letting it leak out in sarcastic snipes.

- **Do you have trouble sharing your feelings?** Then try to open your heart so as to let others in, not feeling the pressure to speak with Shakespearean elegance, just being yourself. Those who love you are not looking for a Pulitzer Prize winning essay, just a window into your soul.

- **Do you wear a mask?** Then try to stop hiding behind what you think will make people like you, and realize that the real you is the real treasure.

- **Do you drink too much?** Then try to control your drinking, or, if your family lovingly tells you that your abusive drinking has caused them pain, then seek treatment so as to get the albatross of alcoholism off your back.

- **Does your pessimism bring everybody down?** Then examine the ideas that control your feelings, replacing negative and unrealistic ones with their more positive counterparts. Try to stop dwelling on what little is wrong, and focus upon what is right, realizing that the glass is often considerably more than half full.

This is not easy, so do not get discouraged, patience and persistence being the words of the day. Whatever your issues, face them, and the enjoyment of ever-increasing happiness will be yours, not only in the New Year, but in all the years to come.

OUR MAP: *The Holidays*

PRINCIPLES and PROBLEMS
How our principles helped solve these problems.

INSECURITY: There are no perfect presents, no perfect parties, and no perfect families, even though every TV special says so.

POWER: Decide how you wish to celebrate the holidays instead of succumbing to the pressure of grandparents to visit, friends to party, or commercials to buy.

SUCCESS: The holidays are a time to reflect on the meaning and direction of your life, not just stuff your face with turkey and open presents.

CHAPTER FOUR

GETTING LOST

Some of the people whom we meet and the challenges that we face while on our journey to happiness can entice us to take a wrong turn, to try an ineffective solution, or to just plain feel overwhelmed. Simply put, we get lost.

And, what is worse, we either do not know it, or just keep on keeping on the wrong path, essentially becoming conditioned by the poor decisions that we continually make, usually due to being too scared or proud to face the truth.

What follows below are some of the common ways in which we can get lost, and some simple ideas as to how to find our way back to a more productive path. We begin by looking at the masks that people wear to hide their insecurity and self-doubt, twisting themselves into psychological pretzels to promote praise and avoid criticism.

Then we look at the pervasive problem of depression in our culture, when we judge that our masks are not working, and that we have just not measured up to the standards that others have imposed on us and that we have gullibly swallowed. Anxiety will be seen as the flip side of depression, it being our nervousness of not being able to continue measuring up before the juggling act fails and all comes crashing down into the black hole of depression.

Finally, our exploration of our clay feet shall continue by looking at other problems over which many people trip, such as frustration, guilt, procrastination, and jealousy. Special attention will be given to the pervasive problems of adultery and addictions.

A. Masks

We shall begin with a general look at what these personas or masks tend to be, and then look in more detail at the more common masks that you will encounter.

1. Hiding Behind Masks

QUESTION: I can't stand people who are fake. They hide behind masks. Why in heaven's name do they do that?

ANSWER

A secret in life is that all people feel insecure. Masks are ineffective solutions to the problem of insecurity, either trying to fool others by pretending to be superior, or tragically fooling yourself by acting inferior.

If only a person could be guided by the principles that we discussed earlier in the book, then the need to wear masks would disappear. Instead of holding onto the power to determine their self-worth, they give that power to others and then nervously await their judgment. Instead of realizing that all people feel insecure, they labor under the mistaken myth of some being very secure and so attempt to pretend to be like them by wearing a mask.

The tragedy of wearing a mask is that if we wear them too long, we find that we cannot remove them. The masks we wear on Halloween, we can take off at the end of the evening. The personality masks that hide who we are become harder to take off as each year passes, as if we begin to believe the web of lies that we have been spinning. Hence, my advice is to take your mask off, realizing that your true self is far more beautiful than any mask, no matter how bejeweled it may be.

So that you may see what lengths to which people go to conceal rather than deal with their insecurities, here are but a few examples of masks people wear everyday:

1. **The Snob**: This person puts himself up by putting you down. They narcissistically throw in your face the fact that they live on the right street, drive the right car, or know the right people, the not-so-subtle implication being that you do not! They often define themselves by what they *have* instead of who they are.

2. **The Workaholic:** This person defines self by what they *do* instead of who they are, compulsively working long hours due to feeling short on self-esteem. They endlessly tell you about how much they have accomplished on their job, what their title is, how many people are under them, or how much they make, the implication being that the firm would fold without them. They have a hard time relaxing, taking work home with them, and even converting fun into work, wanting to shoot the lowest score in golf so as to feel high.

3. **Macho Man:** This person hides their fear of you by making you scared of them. This is yesterday's bully from grade school, who today controls by making you feel uncomfortable, perhaps by yelling or being "in your face" during an argument. When people back down, they feel powerful. But, when people back away, especially a spouse, their paranoid fear of rejection shows itself in jealous accusations of infidelity, and a cynical worldview that is a definite "turn off". The more assertive the spouse becomes, the more abusive the behavior becomes, often escalating to slapping and hitting.

4. **The Martyr:** This person manipulates by feelings, drawing such a "poor me" picture, that you find yourself drawn to doing things for them. However, after the 6th crisis in 2 weeks, you duck when you see them coming, as you see them as a "bottomless pit" of need. As we all want to help others, this person then just moves on to the next "sucker", never realizing that they do not have to act sad to become happy.

5. **Shy Guy:** This person avoids social situations, having to be dragged to a party, where they hover on the fringe of conversations, studying people to discover who is "safe". If either slightly rebuffed or ignored, they retreat to their corner, complaining enough until their spouse reluctantly agrees to go home. While very talented, they often put themselves down, and are overly dismayed if they make a public mistake, each goof reinforcing the decision to hang back for fear of embarrassment.

6. **The Clinger:** This is someone who judges him or herself to be weak, and accordingly, clings to someone else whom they think is strong. They passively allow this person to make important decisions for them, such as buy-

ing a house or car, or determining to which school the children will go. Instead of depending on a mythical hero, they need to discover their own inner worth, and then nervously and gradually stand on their own two feet.

2. The Snob

QUESTION: One of my friends is a real snob. He's always bragging about his business, showing off his new car, or telling me about all the important people he knows. It turns me off, but I don't know how to help him without hurting his feelings. What can I do?

ANSWER

WHAT THEY DO

If you have a friend who is a snob, what you can do is to more fully understand him so as to better help him. The "snob" wants your admiration, hopes for your jealousy, but usually ends up alienating you.

These individuals always know the right people, live in the right neighborhood, drive the right car, and are invited to all the right parties. The not-so-subtle implication is that you do not! Even if they have not been drenched with success as of yet, they proclaim that it is just around the corner. They love to compare, hoping to feel up by making others feel down.

WHY THEY DO IT

This behavior could have one of two causes. *First*, overcritical parenting may have scared your friend that he would not be able to live up to parental expectations, and so he adopts any of a number of symbols of success for protection. *Secondly*, overpermissive parenting may have made him picture a universe with him at the center. When the world imposes limits that parents have not, feelings of insecurity bubble to the surface and up pops all those symbols for the appearance of success.

WHAT YOU CAN DO

The solution involves achieving acceptance of self. You can help your friend by constructively confronting him. He needs to wake up to the fact that bragging, faking feelings, or lying regarding personal deficits pushes away the very person he wants to befriend—you! Trying new behavior and being pleasantly surprised by acceptance and warmth may be enough of a taste to get your friend to try even harder. So, the solution calls for bravery from your friend and assertiveness from you. Good luck.

KEY POINTS

- Insecurity: The snob tries to feel up by making you feel down, pointing out what they *have* that you do not.

- Power: Symbols are used to stave off feelings of not measuring up to overcritical parents or not being overly entitled when overly permissive parents told them that they were.

- Success: Helping them is sensitively confronting arrogance or fake feelings with a deeper picture of who they truly are underneath their mask.

3. The Workaholic

QUESTION: My husband is a workaholic. I am tired of being a married widow! I appreciate his being a good provider, but he is ridiculous. He's never home. I complain and complain, but it does no good. Why does he do it? What can I do?

ANSWER

WHAT THEY DO

The workaholic believes that love is conditional, and that he must work to be accepted, praised, and loved by others. Accordingly, he works long hours, often skips lunch, comes home late for dinner, and then usually brings "catch-up" work home with him. When relaxation is considered justified, he feels such time must be purposeful. So, he is unable to just sit and watch television, tending to balance his checkbook, read a magazine article, or labor over a crossword puzzle at the same time. Vacations are rarely taken, but if they are, rest is converted into work, namely, seeing all the sites, catching the most fish, or perfecting his golf game.

WHY THEY DO IT

How did he get into this mess? At the base, we often find parents who unwittingly taught him that love is conditional, namely, that if he got good grades, cleaned his room, took out the garbage, or got a hit in Little League baseball, that he was "a good boy". While this at first seems harmless enough, it is based on the premise that you are what you do.

Perhaps this becomes clearer if we turn it around. If your son fails a course at school, or even gets arrested, does that make him bad? We must separate the deed from the doer, the sin from the sinner. Of course, we are not going to jump for joy if Junior gets an F, but I hope that we are not going to disown him either. He must realize that win or lose, we still love him. Unfortunately, in our competitive society, we seldom say that, and the child grows up thinking that he must work to prove himself.

WHAT YOU CAN DO

Therefore, to help the workaholic who might be your husband, you must reassure him. He must realize that he is more than what he does, and that even if he makes mistakes, or, God forbid, gets fired, you will still be there for him. He must realize that love is unconditional, and that he is pushing happiness away with both hands, futilely trying to please all the people all the time.

Accepting this message, he must slowly begin to lower his commitments to a more realistic level. He must try to come home on time from work, relax when home, not join too many outside organizations, and, believe it or not, spend some quality time with you and the children. Lastly, you must realize that change is gradual, being patient without nagging if he is trying. Nagging will imply conditional love, and even if he improves, he will do the right thing for the wrong reason, and you will go from being his wife to his taskmaster.

KEY POINTS

- Insecurity: The workaholic works hard to be accepted, praised and loved.
- Power: Overcritical parents made them feel that love was conditional upon performance.
- Success: Helping them is enabling them to see that they are more than the sum of what they do, and that your love for them is unconditional.

4. The Martyr

QUESTION: I have a friend who always plays the martyr. Everything is a disaster. It's always "Oh woe is me!" I try to help, but I feel like I'm drained. Why are people like this?

ANSWER

WHAT THEY DO

The "martyr" is often someone whom we are scared to ask, "How are you today?" We know that we are doomed to listen to a lengthy tale of woe, and so, laden with guilt, either do not bother to ask or duck the other way when we see them coming. What they fail to see is that, while you feel sorry for them at first, they "turn you off" in the long run. After you have helped someone with his or her 6th crisis in 2 weeks, you begin to label the martyr "a pest".

WHY THEY DO IT

Usually, they come from a background where they did not receive sufficient attention, and so have decided to manipulate your attention by their exaggerations. That does not necessarily mean that their parents purposely neglected them, just that they felt neglected. In other cases, parents may have awarded attention due to the histrionics of their child, giving in being easier than addressing the acting out behavior of their child.

So, to continue getting attention, the martyr may twist the history of their past to their advantage, presenting a Cinderella story complete with wicked stepsisters, hoping that you fall neatly into the role of the prince and rescue them by providing a fairy tale love. Yet, no matter how much love you give, you end up with the frustrating feeling that you are trying to fill a bottomless pit.

WHAT YOU CAN DO

Get beyond the behavior to its underlying meaning. Help the person to realize that your love does not have to be forced, that you are willing to give it freely.

Then, show your friend that his or her behavior is not pulling you towards them, but instead pushing you away. If the person wants attention, they can get it by stating rather than exaggerating the problem. Your friend must realize, however, that you too have limits, and that you cannot replace their parents. The person must let go of the past, not try to relive it. This needs to be explained carefully to your friend so that the person does not see criticism of their behavior as rejection of them.

KEY POINTS

- Insecurity: The martyr believes that love will not come to them unless they force it by exaggerating their feelings to get your attention.
- Power: They may feel that they were neglected by their parents, or may have learned that attention comes from acting out, not relaxing and letting their inner worth attract others.
- Success: Help them to realize that your love does not have to be forced, being based instead upon who they are, not how they act.

5. The Pessimist

QUESTION: My husband is a pessimist. He's always negative. I'm exhausted trying to bring him up, and now he's beginning to bring me down. What would make someone act like that? How can I help lift his spirits?

ANSWER

Being a pessimist is not necessarily a mask, but rather an overarching belief that that can infect any mask. The person is always negative, exhausting those close to him or her in trying to uplift their spirits.

Why do they do it? There are many reasons; here are three possible explanations and ways to address each issue.

1. **LOWERING EXPECTATIONS:**
   - *Problem*: If his parents unwittingly made him think that getting their love was conditional upon getting an A in school or a hit in baseball, then being a pessimist is a defensive posture, lowering expectations so as to lower criticism if he does not "deliver". Often, a pessimist will say that they "hope for the best, but expect the worst".
   - *Solution*: Helping him would mean showing him that your love is unconditional, and that he does not have to prove himself to you each day. This does not mean that you cannot give him constructive criticism, just that you must not allow him to think that his internal worth depends upon your external praise.

2. **GETTING ATTENTION:**
   - *Problem*: If he feels that he never got enough attention as a child, he may complain about life so as to manipulate others like you to give him TLC. As most people want to feel good by helping others, this usually works for a while, until he is seen as such a "downer" that people avoid him like the plague.
   - *Solution*: Helping him is showing him that his game plan has blown up in his face. Instead of getting attention, he is driving people away in droves. Again, underlying this behavior is a lack of self-esteem. So, reflecting back to him his good qualities will help him wake up to his inner worth.

3. **PAST EXPERIENCES:**

    - *__Problem__*: He may have genuinely had many negative experiences in his life that have colored the way in which he views the world. If he was abused as a child, divorced or downsized as an adult, or all of the above, he may well assume that past experiences will simply be repeated in the future.

    - *__Solution__*: Helping him is not to deny the negative portions of his life, but to get him to look at the whole picture. Yes, the glass is half empty, but it is also half full. For example, he has you! Ask him why you love him. Is it because you are stupid, or perhaps that you see something in him that he does not? Of course, the question is rhetorical, and the hope is that he can begin to see his value mirrored back to him through your love.

Finally, let me say that life is hard. It is easy to focus upon the negative. Therefore, if someone gets into the habit of doing so, it is difficult to change. So, while persistently urging the pessimist to change, be patient.

6. Real Men Don't Cry

QUESTION: *My husband is like an emotional rock. I know he's a caring guy, but he never cries. He always has to act like he's strong, but that leaves me more and more alone. Why do men have such a problem with emotions?*

ANSWER

Another myth that strangles intimacy for men is that "real men don't cry." Many men see expressing feelings, especially crying, as a sign of weakness. Their fear is that men will ridicule them, and women will reject them.

I recently saw a couple where the wife was urging her husband to share his feelings. When he finally did, courageously speaking with tears in his eyes, she stared at him with disgust and exclaimed, "And I thought that I married a real man!" Needless to say, any further motivation of his to "let it all hang out" went down in flames.

To attack this problem, we must attack the myth that a man is weak if he expresses his emotions. What must it be like to be married to an "emotional rock"? Whether your husband is the strong, silent type or someone who intellectualizes his feelings, giving you a computer printout of 7.5 reasons for loving you, the end result is the same, namely, you are starving to death emotionally. The pain that you are feeling is proof positive that holding feelings in has let the air out of your marriage.

So, how do you get him to change? Here are **three ideas**.

1. **BE REALISTIC**: Make sure that you have changed, that you are not like the wife I just described. Both you and your husband must realize that the "real man" images of Dirty Harry, Rambo, The Terminator, or The Duke are just that—images. They are imaginary, and, even if they were real, they would need intense therapy a lot more than idol worship.

2. **BE PATIENT**: Realize that your husband may have had some rather deep conditioning in his family. I had a client once whose father died when he was a boy. Kneeling before his father's casket at the wake, he began to have tears running down his cheeks. His much older brother came up to him and whispered, "If you can't control yourself, you won't be allowed to stay!" It took that boy years to reverse the pattern that he was taught, even though he knew it was wrong.

3. **<u>BE PERSISTENT</u>**: Practice does make perfect. My advice to couples is that they get into the habit of setting aside one hour per week to talk. That time span enables you to go deeper than the normal "How was your day?" conversation. Also, try to enjoy it. This is not a grilling under the fluorescent lights in the kitchen, but rather a romantic talk in the living room with soft music and dimmed lighting to set the mood. When couples smirk and remind me that they have children, I simply challenge them to get creative. If you are too tired when the kids are in bed, consider using your DVD player and a favorite Disney disk to occupy the kids. Hard—yes. Impossible—no. Your reward will be the marriage that you have always wanted.

OUR MAP: *Masks*

PRINCIPLES and PROBLEMS
How our principles helped solve these problems.

INSECURITY: Accept that we all feel insecure instead of hiding behind a mask, either trying to fool others by acting superior or fooling yourself by acting inferior.

FURTHER READING

- Berne, Eric, Games People Play: The Basic Handbook of Transactional Analysis, New York, Random House, 1964.
- Masterson, James F., The Search for the Real Self, New York, The Free Press, 1988.
- Peck, M. Scott, The People of the Lie, New York, Simon & Schuster, 1983.

B. Emotional Derailment

Masks are a futile attempt to cope with feeling insecure by either denying insecurity (*a superiority complex*) or giving in to it (*an inferiority complex*). While many people wear masks, they are poor solutions so riddled with cracks of reality that they not only do not fool the average person, but they also cannot hold back the floodgates of truth from the wearer.

Then a person must emotionally react either to their not having lived up to the expectations of others, in which case they become depressed, or to the immense pressure they feel to measure up, in which case they become anxious. As these two conditions affect millions of people, we shall look at each, and then at other related problems. For instance, we shall see that in attempting to measure up, a person can emotionally react to the pressure of performing before (*worry*), during (*frustration*), or after (*guilt and shame*) it.

The correlation with our principles is simple. If a person could take back the power to define their worth instead of giving it to others, and then be patient with their growth, realizing it is a process instead of a product, and that all people are insecure and struggling too, then I think many of these problems could be either avoided or greatly ameliorated. Thus, a consideration of how a person becomes derailed emotionally while traveling down the road to happiness will put flesh on the bones of our principles, better enabling you to see how central they truly are.

1. Depression

a. The What, Why & How of Depression

QUESTION: *I have been feeling down in the dumps for some time. Could you explain what depression is, and what can be done about it?*

ANSWER: My answer is in three parts.

WHAT

1. **DEFINITION**: Depression is *a gap between who you are (ego) and who you think you should be (ego ideal).* When you think that you are a few "shoulds" short, and, therefore, do not measure up, you get depressed.

2. **SYMPTOMS**: As depression is anger turned in, many of the symptoms essentially punish you for being "bad". Most common are:

    *   *Difficulty sleeping*, where you wake up in the middle of the night and cannot get back to sleep.

    *   Or, where you *do not feel like eating*, and have recently lost over 10 pounds.

    *   Others are *difficulty concentrating*, as you are dwelling on your failures, often accompanied by

    *   *Crying* and *a pessimistic attitude*.

    *   You may also *withdraw from friends and fun*, nothing seeming to pick up your spirits.

    *   The ultimate, and most upsetting, sign of anger at self is *suicidal thinking*.

WHY

DYNAMICS: Who we think we should be is largely determined by parents. Often, they unwittingly set unrealistic expectations for their children, communicating that love is conditional upon getting a home run in baseball, good marks in school, a good job, or a good spouse. So, when you get an F in spelling in fourth grade, or do not get that promotion you were counting on at work, you feel like you failed, and get depressed.

As the connection to pleasing your parents is long lost, you probably have transferred your desire to please to a substitute parent, such as a teacher, employer, or spouse. Should you fail to please this person, or should that person no longer be there to praise you, you get depressed.

HOW

1. __COUNSELING__:

- Overcoming depression is *a matter of accepting yourself, of looking for validation from within rather than from without.* This does not mean abandoning your goals, but rather striving for them because you "want to", not because you "have to".

- Ironically, your negative thinking is probably so ingrained that you would fight your therapist, claiming that you are, indeed, a failure.

- The therapist then does not try to balance out a negative parent by telling you how good you are, for that only means that your self-worth still comes from outside yourself. Instead, the therapist elicits your own inner strength, getting you to challenge your negative thoughts, and replace them with more positive ones.

2. __MEDICATION__:

- When you are depressed, there is a decrease in the brain of neurotransmitters, such as serotonin. What that means is that you think slower, tending to get stuck in your negative thoughts, dwelling on them. *Antidepressant medication increases these neurotransmitters so as to help you think quicker and get "unstuck".*

- However, these medications often take three to four weeks before they begin to work. A rule of thumb that I often give to people is that it takes one month before you notice any difference, and two months before you notice the full difference. As people notice the side effects right away, but have not yet benefited from the primary effects of the medication, they often discontinue the medication if there is not someone helping them to be patient.

- Another frustration is that not every medicine works for every person. Hard as it is, try not to get discouraged, as there are many antidepressants, so should one not work, just call you doctor who may either increase your dosage or try a second medication after slowly taking you off the first.

- And, do not fall into the trap of thinking that the medication "cures" depression. While depression does indicate a chemical imbalance, and while the medication thereby does allow your mind to work more effectively, nonetheless, your mind must still do the work of uncovering the causes of depression, and then of assessing and dispelling negative thinking. To attempt to fight depression with only medication is like trying to fight with one arm tied behind your back.

- Lastly, remember that treatment helps you to learn how to deal with depression, but dealing with it is a lifetime process, not a quick fix.

So, if you are one of the millions of Americans who suffer from depression, realize that you can ease your suffering by beginning treatment. Facing a problem does not make you weak. Instead, try to live as I do by the motto that the admission of weakness is the beginning of strength.

And finally, while I am a therapist and thus focus upon the traditional way to combat depression, I do not wish to imply that what I have written is the only way. For instance, there are other holistic approaches to treating depression that offer relief.

Even in the treatment itself, I combine counseling and medication with simple things that a person can do during the week. As becoming happier and less depressed involves loving and accepting one's self more, I suggest that a person consciously do something each day strictly for him- or herself. Perhaps that will be watching a favorite TV show, taking a long bath, going on a walk, or reading a book that just plain gives pleasure instead of always being "meaningful". It is very simple and need not cost a penny, but it does take small steps to loving one's self and sets the stage for harder, bigger steps later.

b. Turning Bad Ideas Good

QUESTION: *I've got a friend who's depressed. He's always so negative, as if look-*
ing at life through a dark and gloomy filter. How can I get through to him?

ANSWER

People who are depressed suffer from a "domino effect". Ideas trigger feelings,
which in turn trigger behaviors. To help a depressed person, we need to turn
bad ideas good. This is what is called "Cognitive Therapy", the focus being on
our cognitions, our ideas.

A. **THINKING:** Negative ideas bring people down because they are distorted.
    Helping a depressed friend is helping him find and correct the distortion.
    Let me give you some examples.

    1. **MAGNIFYING:** Flubbing a job interview neither makes you an idiot,
        nor does it mean that all future interviews are hopeless and futile wastes
        of your time. Try not to blow things out of proportion, but instead
        realize that a mistake today can be corrected tomorrow. Life is often
        more gray than black and white.

    2. **DWELLING:** While everyone has weaknesses, why focus exclusively on
        them? Instead, regain perspective by taking the blinders off, and not
        discounting your positive qualities and accomplishments. This is not
        an internal "snow job", but rather seeing that the glass is really a lot
        more than half-full.

    3. **ASSUMING:** Predicting that people will not like you, and that you will
        never find a job or fall in love condemns you to a self-fulfilling proph-
        ecy where you are sitting at home alone on a Saturday night all because
        you have projected your own self-doubt onto others. Try to give peo-
        ple, and yourself, a chance.

    4. **BLAMING:** Playing ping pong with blame is again all-or-nothing
        thinking, where your anger can point inwards to see yourself as a
        "loser" or outwards to see others as "cruel". Stop labeling yourself and

others, and instead see your thinking as depriving you and them from opportunities to grow and be happy.

B.   TREATING: Helping your friend can be done in the following ways.

1.   **EVIDENCE**: Ask your friend to prove his point, for there will not be sufficient evidence to justify his generalizations.

2.   **QUESTIONS**: Ride his irrational, inconsistent, and negative thoughts until they crash. Asking him probing questions gets him to do the work of examining his own ideas, with the hope that his innate intelligence will help him to abandon ideas that now look foolish.

3.   **FANTASY**: Get him to imagine and confront his worst fears, helping him realize that he is really facing a paper tiger. If he can deal with the worst that could happen, then dealing with less than that should be a cinch.

4.   **OPENNESS**: As this is your friend, show him how you have faced your own demons, dealing with self-doubt, anger, or shyness. Then, he will not be alone.

5.   **SUBSTITUTION**: Finally, get your friend to replace his negative idea with a more positive and accurate one, which will gradually result in happier feelings and more productive behavior.

2. Anxiety

Anxiety and depression are opposite sides of the same coin. The anxious person worries that he or she may not measure up to the standards of others now self imposed, whereas the depressed person thinks that the game is already over, that they have failed to measure up and hence hang their heads in shame.

a. The What, Why & How of Anxiety

QUESTION: I had a friend who went to the Emergency Room thinking that he was having a heart attack. It turned out there was nothing wrong with him physically. It was just anxiety. I thought that was just normal nervousness, but I guess there's more to it than that. Could you help me understand it better?

ANSWER: Millions suffer from anxiety, so your friend is not alone.

WHAT

1. **DEFINITION**: Anxiety is being apprehensive or worrying about what may happen. A little is useful, helping you study for a test, or making sure that you pack everything for a trip. Too much for too long is not good, paralyzing your ability to function.

2. **SYMPTOMS**:
    a. *Psychological*: Fearfully dwelling and ruminating about what could go wrong.
    b. *Physical*: Difficulty breathing, a lump in your throat, an upset stomach, diarrhea, a stiff neck, headache, rapid heartbeat, dizziness, cold sweats, trembling, restless sleeping, and nightmares, to name but a few.

3. **SOME TYPES**:
    a. *Generalized Anxiety Disorder*: Continual symptoms, but less intense.
    b. *Panic Disorder*: Occasional symptoms, but intense and unpredictable, where the person thinks that he or she may be having a heart attack or "going crazy".
    c. *Obsessive-Compulsive Disorder (OCD)*: Fighting off obsessive thoughts of potential failure or criticism with compulsive behaviors such as hand-washing,

checking to see if doors are locked or if a report has mistakes. *Felix Unger* of yesteryear and *Monk* of today exemplify this problem.

    d. *Phobic Disorder*: Subconsciously encapsulating general fears into a specific object (snakes, heights, flying, closed spaces, etc.) that a person then tries to avoid, this being your mind's effort to stuff your fears into Pandora's Box.

WHY

<u>CAUSES</u>:

- They are both *physical*, such as a chemical imbalance, and *psychological*, such as a fear of failure, criticism or rejection.
- The roots of these fears can be
  - o Overcritical parents who imply that love is conditional upon performance, or
  - o Overprotective parents who imply that we are too weak to deal with a very scary world.
- Finally, our competitive society, which promotes the aggressive and belittles the fainthearted, pours gas all over the tinderbox of self-doubt.

HOW

TREATMENT: involves both medication and counseling.

1. **<u>MEDICATION</u>**: These provide temporary relief, but, as they can be addictive, should be only used as needed. Some medications include: valium, librium, and xanax.

2. **<u>COUNSELING</u>**: This consists of:
    - Examining the causes of anxiety, and then
    - Behaviorally climbing a ladder from the least (telling a waitress that the medium steak you ordered is rare) to the most stressful events (telling your spouse to grow up or get out). Also, it is important to
    - Look at the negative ideas ("I blew the interview! I'll never get a job.") controlling our feelings, and convert them into more positive ones ("I'll learn from my mistakes and do better next time."). Otherwise, imagine that if you think that you are going to "blow" the interview,

your anxiety during the interview will be sky high. A calmer idea will produce a calmer mood during the interview. Finally,

- Your unconditional love and belief in a person shows them that you mean what you say, namely, that they can rest assured of your love instead of worrying that too many flubs will result in your rejection of them.

Again, my intent here is only to show you the clinical treatment for anxiety, fully aware that there are many other ways to relieve anxiety, the benefit of a massage, for instance, being known to us all.

b. Panic Attacks

QUESTION: *My friend suffers from panic attacks. She is so scared of having one that she imposes on others, which has strained both her marriage and our friendship. There is really nothing all that bad in her life. Can't she just snap out of it?*

ANSWER

Approximately 1 out of 6 suffers from an anxiety disorder, the most common and perhaps the scariest being the panic attack. It is a greatly misunderstood condition, from which recovery takes time. Therefore, a person cannot just "snap out of it".

1. **DEFINITION**: A panic attack involves the sudden and unexpected onset of intense anxiety, typified by sweaty palms, trembling, a rapid heartbeat, tightness of the chest, dizziness, and a fear of losing control, having a heart attack or going crazy. To the person suffering, it seems unending, but it usually lasts only a few minutes. If differs from other anxiety disorders, which are less intense, last longer, and are more predictable.

2. **EFFECT**:
   a. *On Self*: The fear of losing control and having another attack lead people to avoid places and social situations where escape would be difficult. They become prisoners of their fear, shrinking their world to expand their comfort level.
   b. *On Others*: Often, the spouse or a close friend is asked to do the grocery shopping, be the sole parent at school functions, and be a constant chauffeur for the family. Over time, resentment understandably builds.

3. **CAUSES**: They are complex, but seem to be both psychological and physical. The personality of the individual seems to be an overly responsible, perfectionistic worrier, who is very sensitive to criticism. Parents may have been overprotective worriers or overcritical yellers, or a combination of both. However, in some cases, heredity rather than parenting may be the cause.

4. **TREATMENT**: Effective relief requires a package approach, probably involving three elements: counseling, medication, and a self-help group.
   a. *Counseling* would help the person to understand the nature and roots of the problem, as well as how their own fear and vivid imaginations of "what if"

situations trigger further attacks. Gradually, the person would be desensitized to stressful situations (shopping, driving, being alone), keeping a journal so as to study their own reactions. Improvement would also show an increase in self-confidence and assertiveness, while a decrease in rigid perfectionism and self-criticism.

Therapy would also need to include significant others, primarily family, but also very close friends, to understand the secondary impact of the panic attacks on them, and the need for them to patiently encourage increasing independence by decreasing their own co-dependence.

b. _Medication_ would be to "get over the hump", but not a crutch upon which the person may become addicted. This does not mean that ongoing use of those medications would stop, just that they would be used carefully.

c. _Self-Help Groups_ are effective because the person no longer feels alone, and can learn different ways of coping. While everyone has the same problem, everyone has experimented with different solutions. Hence, even if a person sits there like a stone not talking, they can still learn just by simply listening to others explain what does and does not work.

c. Worry
The What Ifs

QUESTION: *I worry all the time. My wife says I have a bad case of the "what ifs". I'm tired of being paralyzed by my own anxiety. Can you help me?*

ANSWER

Some people, while not having a diagnosable anxiety disorder, tend to torture themselves with worry. Worry is a disease of the imagination. To control it, you try to prepare for all the "what ifs", but unfortunately you can "what if" yourself to death, squeezing all the pleasure out of the moment by pessimistically imagining what could go wrong instead of optimistically hoping it will go right.

Not all worry is bad. If you did not worry about passing a test in school, finishing projects on time at work, or getting gas before a trip or groceries before a snowstorm, you would end up in trouble. But, while good worry leads to constructive action, bad worry leads to paralysis. So, here are some ways to increase your power so as to decrease your worrying.

1. **TALK:** Instead of worrying alone which only leads to your imagination spiraling out of control, talk to someone whom you trust and with whom you can share your concerns. This person can serve as a safety check, helping bring you back to earth when you are "making a mountain out of a molehill".

2. **THINK:** Instead of wallowing in what could go wrong, think of what you could do to solve the problem. While I realize that your mind will search for the perfect solution, accept the fact that there isn't one!

3. **ACT:** Armed with a plan, put it into action. Worried about your health, get a physical. Worried about work, tell your wife that you will be home a little later and get a head start on the project.

4. **THERAPY:** The above sounds simple, but my guess is that you will need more help in the form of counseling.

    a. *WHY:* First, this will show you the roots of your worrying.

- Perhaps you had overcritical parents who made you worry that love was conditional upon good grades.

- Perhaps one of your parents imbued you with their own negative thinking with such adages as "Hope for the best, but expect the worst." So, to cope, you have picked up the gauntlet of being a perfectionist, who obsessively plans to avoid harm only to find yourself mired in a maze of negative and cynical thinking.

b. _HOW_: Secondly, you can explore how you think, exposing those automatic, knee-jerk patterns of thinking that cascade you downwards to a day of doom and gloom. Gradually, you will learn how to extract the negative, unrealistic thought and replace it with a more positive and realistic one.

5. **MEDICATION**: As I have said before, medications are a two-edged sword. While medications like valium or xanax can get you over the hump when very upset, they are addictive, and you must not overly rely upon them. As many worriers are also depressed, the drug paxil is a safer alternative in treating depression and stress with less risk of dependency.

6. **PRAYER**: A relationship with God can bathe you in unconditional love, and help you see the forest for the trees, the big picture helping you worry less about the little picture.

7. **SELF-CARE**: If you are pooped, you will be more prone to worry. So, get enough sleep, eat well, and exercise.

8. **DISTRACTION**: While the above sounds great, you will still worry. So, when those thoughts inevitably invade your mind, distract yourself from worrying by getting up, watching TV, eating a snack, taking a walk, listening to the radio, or anything that will momentarily help you stop yourself in your tracks rather then let you sink into a sticky web of "what ifs".

3. Frustration

QUESTION: How do you deal with frustration? When things don't go my way, I really get bent out of shape.

ANSWER

Worry is anticipating that something *will go* wrong. Frustration occurs when something *is going* wrong, your expectations crashing headlong into a reality that just plain does not match. Let us discuss two situations.

First, imagine a situation over which you have no control. If you expect your drive home to take thirty minutes, and it really takes ninety minutes, you get frustrated. What can you do? You can fume about the "idiot" whose reckless driving inconveniently tied up traffic with an accident, yelling to yourself that "life sucks", and inching your car from lane to lane in a vain attempt to "speed things up". However, the end result is that your blood pressure soars, and your unsuspecting spouse is in for a nightmare of an evening.

Instead, you can calm down, accept the reality that life has its share of bumps, turn your radio to a favorite station, and try to enjoy some unplanned "down" time. When you arrive home, you are not exactly "a happy camper", but you will not be allowing something over which you had no control to destroy your evening over which you do.

Secondly, imagine a situation where you have much more say in what occurs. On another evening, you arrive home, hoping to take a warm shower, have a cold beer, and relax watching TV. However, your wife has had an equally rough day with the children, and wants you to not only show her understanding and empathy, but also to give her a much-needed break—immediately! Your reaction? You could blow your stack, berating her for being "an insensitive clod" in not giving you a second to catch your breath. Or, you could "cave" and do what she expects, all the while muttering sarcastic, backbiting comments meant to not-so-subtly teach her a lesson for not living up to your expectations.

Instead, you and she could sit down and think out a solution to this common problem. Oh, yes, that would probably be after "blowing it" and learning from your mistakes, but my point is that this learning would involve having the expectations of you and your spouse match the reality that you are facing. Both needs are realistic, but cannot be accomplished simultaneously. Taking control of the situation means neither blaming your spouse, nor condemning yourself to a world of frustration, but rather facing the normal limitations of life, listening to one another, and compromising.

In both situations, frustration can actually awaken you to a need for creativity and change, and, instead of suffering from angina and a divorce, you can learn to not only manage stress, but also actually turn a potential negative into a very real positive.

KEY POINTS

- If you have no control over a situation, calm down, realizing there is nothing you can do.
- If you have some control over a situation, talk out a mutually agreed solution or compromise, accepting that no solution is perfect.

4. Guilt

QUESTION: My best friend never admits when he's wrong. It's always somebody else's fault. Why can't he just be honest and accept his blame?

ANSWER

If you are keeping track of how these stumbling blocks to finding happiness are related, worry anticipates problems before they occur, frustration bemoans setbacks while they occur, and guilt accepts blame after they occur.

However, unlike the other two, guilt is not always bad. The stumbling block to your search for happiness is when people either refuse to accept blame, or when guilt turns into shame.

1. **FEAR OF REJECTION**: Acceptance of blame is a lost art. Why? Well, remember one of our principles, namely, that all people feel somewhat insecure. The most insecure person fears being exposed as a fake, and so hides behind a mask of superiority. As accepting blame means taking off that mask and risking rejection, some people become masters of deceit.

Once confronted, they may deny having anything to do with it, or try to rationalize their way out of a jam, bombarding you with excuses as to why they did what they did. Finally, they may project the blame to someone else, angrily proclaiming their innocence by stating that it was "the other guy's fault", or that they are the victims of abusive parents, a demanding boss, or a "bitchy wife".

2. **GUILT AND SHAME**: Rather than ducking blame, guilt is an intellectual admission of doing something wrong; it is taking responsibility for your own behavior. Shame, however, is an emotional response to guilt, a feeling of having failed to live up to your potential.

Feeling humbled by your shame, the hope is that you face your problem and grow, but others try all the more to hide their blame, fearing being spotted as a "loser". But, the road to growth is paved with honesty, so that when you courageously reveal the "real you", you can be pleasantly surprised to discover that people like you less for what you do, and more for who you are.

But, if shame makes you feel that you are no longer worthy of another shot at happiness, then you become stuck. You need to free yourself up by forgiving yourself. If you are guilty, you may think that you are not worthy of forgiveness, but as you will see, we all are.

3. **<u>FORGIVENESS</u>**: You are forgiven not only because the person forgiving you is nice, but also and primarily because you have the potential (the power) to change. Who you are is more than the sum of what you do. So, once you admit being wrong, you have taken the first step in the right direction. Hiding the truth by denying guilt only puts up a wall between you and others, condemning you to the isolation that you wanted to avoid in the first place.

4. **<u>CREATING A CONSCIENCE</u>**: If you have a friend who is dodging guilt, he may also dodge talking to someone prone to tell him to face the truth. To get him to listen to you, you must first lay a foundation to your relationship by being accepting, nonjudgmental, and empathic. This does not mean approving of sinful behavior (*what he did*), but does show your recognition that your friend can change (*who he is*). Harsh, "fire and brimstone" sermons only result in resistance and defensiveness. Your friend needs to see that adhering to social norms will bring him happiness and closeness with others, not simply pleasing his parents, spouse, or you.

You enable your friend to work through his growth by asking him questions that draw out his own thinking, and, thereby, making him own his answers. The ideas become his versus yours, as they are not pumped into him by a stern lecture, but drawn out of his own thinking. You help him harness his own power to grow by helping him see the consequences of his behavior. If he refuses to cooperate, the consequences of his resistance will be his also, the punishment for being selfish being to remain selfish, divided off from you, his good friend.

5. Procrastination

QUESTION: Why do people procrastinate? When I ask my husband to help around the house, he promises but then drags his feet. I have to continually remind and prod him. At work, this has cost him promotions. Why in God's name does he do it?

ANSWER

A final example of emotional derailment would be the problem of procrastination. Why do people do that? I have found that there are two reasons: **fear & anger.**

1. **FEAR:** In the first instance, someone might delay doing something for fear that, once it was done, someone else might criticize or laugh at them. Think back to the first time that you stepped out onto a dance floor, or when you dared raise your hand in class to give an opinion, and you begin to get the picture of what the procrastinator fears. Now add in overcritical parents with high expectations, and a competitive society with a win-lose orientation, and you have all the ingredients for a person with one hand on the doorknob ready to escape and the other on a bottle of Pepto-Bismol for their upset stomach.

2. **ANGER:** The second cause is suppressed anger. The frustration you feel defines one of the purposes for the behavior of your husband, namely, not only to run away from stress, but also to punish you for pushing him towards it. While you did not intend to push, that is, nevertheless, how he feels, carrying on a game originally begun with his parents. Scared to express his anger directly, he does so indirectly, with a host of excuses why this or that did not get done on time.

HOW CAN YOU HELP?

By noticing the problem without being critical, you can get him to talk. By listening to his fear of criticism and anger at being pushed, you can get to the underlying problem of poor self-esteem. But, do not ignore the problem, as that only reinforces it, unwittingly conveying that your husband does not have what it takes to do the job on time. The whole point of my answer is—he does!

OUR MAP: *Emotional Derailment*

PRINCIPLES and PROBLEMS
How our principles helped solve these problems.

<u>INSECURITY</u>: All people are insecure and struggling, so do not chase the ghost of perfect happiness by pleasing a person or possessing a thing.

<u>POWER</u>: Do not twist yourself into a pretzel to become what others think you should be, but accept and rejoice in who you are.

<u>SUCCESS</u>: Grow by learning to become closer and more loving of others empowered by a belief in the potential of yourself.

FURTHER READING

Depression

- Beck, Aaron T., et al., <u>Cognitive Therapy of Depression</u>, New York, Guilford Press, 1987.

- Beck, Judith S., <u>Cognitive Therapy with Children and Adolescents</u>, 2nd Ed., New York, Guilford Press, 2006.

- Burns, David D., <u>The Feeling Good Handbook</u>, New York, Plume, 1999.

- Knaus, William J. <u>The Cognitive Behavioral Workbook</u>, Oakland, CA, New Harbinger Publications, 2006.

- Williams, J. Mark G., John D. Teasdale, Zindel V. Segal, and Jon Kabot-Zinn, <u>The Mindful Way through Depression: Freeing Yourself from Chronic Unhappiness</u>, New York, Guilford Press, 2007.

Anxiety

- Barlow, David, <u>Anxiety & Its Disorders: The Nature and Treatment of Anxiety and Panic</u>, 2nd Ed., New York, Guilford Press, 2004.

- Beck, Aaron T., Gary Emery, and Ruth L. Greenberg, <u>Anxiety Disorders and Phobias: A Cognitive Perspective</u>, New York, Basic Books, 1985.

- Gyoerkoe, Kevin L. and Pamela S. Wiegartz, <u>10 Simple Solutions to Worry: How to Calm Your Mind, Relax Your Budget & Reclaim Your Life</u>, Oakland, CA, New Harbinger Publications, 2006.

- Hallowell, Edward M., <u>Worry: Hope and Help for A Common Condition</u>, New York, Ballantine Books, 1997.

- Helgoe, Laurie E., Laura R. Wilhelm and Martin J. Kommer, <u>The Anxiety Answer Book: Professional, Reassuring Answers to Your Most Pressing Questions</u>, Naperville, IL, Sourcebooks, Inc., 2005.

- Illman, John, <u>Beat Panic & Anxiety: The Complete Guide to Understanding and Tackling Anxiety Disorders</u>, London, Cassell Illustrated, 2004.

Guilt

- Carrell, Susan, <u>Escape Toxic Guilt</u>, New York, McGraw Hill, 2008.

C. Relational Fallout

When a person emotionally derails, there are always relational issues. Treatment is seen as helping not only the person coming for counseling, but also his or her family as well. To see one without the other is not to address the full issue.

But, in addition to the conditions just discussed, there are two others that directly impact a couple: jealousy and adultery.

- The jealous person tries to cope with feeling insecure by controlling their spouse; often, the spouse becomes defensive and the real issue of the jealous person's self-doubt is lost in the whirlwind of blaming.

- The adulterer sees happiness as a product and reaches out for more quantity only to find himself frustrated because happiness is a process aimed at increasing the quality of one's life.

Again, if only these people would honestly face their own insecurity and understand happiness as a process, they would avoid a world of pain for themselves and others. Those simple principles with which we began this book then are seen as more and more important. Traveling on your journey without them condemns you to a host of problems that will push happiness away, whereas armed with them, your search becomes increasingly more productive.

1. Jealousy

QUESTION: *My husband is a jealous nut! He thinks that every man is attracted to me, and more than occasionally accuses me of flirting. That is so insulting. What can I do to get him to be less jealous?*

ANSWER

Let me begin by saying that getting your husband to stop being jealous means getting him to start being more honest. Most jealous men doubt their self-worth. They usually hide behind a macho mask, hoping their bravado will distract you from noticing their fear of rejection. While they may cause you to be afraid of them, they are really scared of you.

To control their fear, they try to control you. Their logic is that if you are home, then you have no chance to compare them with other men, discover that you are "stuck with a loser", and leave. So, they may ask that you not work, or that you wait until they can come with you to the mall or grocery store. As this is generally impossible, they may become detectives, asking you to account for where you were and what you did. As their fear increases, so too do the accusations, often escalating from accusing you of flirting to having affairs.

Many women make the mistake of endlessly defending their behavior instead of looking into the soul of their husband. And, even when some women bravely ask their husbands what is wrong, they usually run head on into that macho mask.

But that is what you must do. You must consistently encourage your husband to reveal his innermost fears. While he will try to resist by defiant silence or childish blowups, you must lovingly insist that this issue be faced. This does not mean nagging him, nor pursuing him from room to room, but tenderly urging him to come to you. When he does, listen carefully, do not interrupt, and be empathic.

While you can reassure him of your love, remember that the focus must be on him. Therefore, get him to see himself through your eyes. Help him to recall those fine qualities that drew you to him in the first place. And whenever he slips and accuses you, sternly tell him that behavior is unacceptable, and again talk regarding his inner worth.

Is that hard? Yes. Is it impossible? No. But, without facing the issue, his abuse will increase, and your marriage will die. So, a little assertion now will save you from a big divorce later.

<u>KEY POINTS</u>

- <u>Insecurity</u>: A jealous person doubts their self-worth and fears rejection. To control their fear, they try to control you, keeping you away from others so as to keep you from comparing them with others.
- <u>Power</u>: Helping them is not defending yourself, but getting them to address their self-doubt. The more they begin believing in themselves, the less jealous they become.

2. Adultery

Another way of dealing with too much criticism and not enough love is to hopefully find a more accepting and nurturing person in a spouse. But, if that person is gradually seen as a carbon copy of emotionally stingy or stringent parents, having clay feet that fall woefully short of providing the full happiness that is desired, then some turn out of their marriage instead of in, resorting to a roving eye for that elusive, special someone who can finally give them all that their heart desires.

As you will see, the problem is thinking that happiness comes from outside ourselves instead of from within, and that the gifts of any present spouse could ever make up for the past mistakes of parents, intentional or not.

The two articles that follow, however, do not posit that an unhealthy marriage should be endured, just faced. Without confronting the problematic marriage first, the affair creates a second problem by illogically putting the cart in front of the horse, often resulting in more pain than cure.

a. Having an Affair

QUESTION: My husband is having an affair with a younger woman. After all the years of being faithful to him and raising our children, this is how he repays me. While I'm crying myself to sleep every night, he seems to be having a ball! Why is life so unfair?

ANSWER

Adultery is widespread in our culture. So too is the myth that goes with it, namely, that you can have your cake and eat it too, that two persons are better than one, or that the spouse having the affair is having a ball.

To understand my point, you must understand marriage. As we saw earlier in this book, marriage is defined by your marital vow, your promise to be true to each other, to continually help each other grow, no matter what comes your way. Your vow is like a protective bubble, keeping interference out and intensity in; you become so intimate with each other that you lovingly help each other grow, gently pointing out weaknesses in one another which you are willing to help your spouse conquer.

Your husband has lost the healing power of that intimacy. Perhaps he doubts his self-worth, and is flattered by the attention of a "younger" woman. Perhaps he is a workaholic who refuses to listen to your advice to work less and relax more, and is comforted in the arms of "a more understanding woman". Whatever is the cause, my point is that he may be running away from himself. While he may seem to be having the time of his life, by not facing his problem, he is condemned to continue living it.

By "fooling around", he loses the intensity of his relationship with you. He cannot simultaneously relate to two women without watering down the power of his relationship. This point is so clear to me that I never allow marriage counseling to begin until the person having the affair ends it. This is not because I am mean, but because the counseling will not otherwise work. If your husband can duck his growth by running to someone who will tell him what he wants to hear, his relationship with you will be stripped of its power. The counseling process will be doomed before it starts.

However, you must now look deep into your own soul. Adultery is not only a problem, but it is also a symptom of a problem in your marriage. Perhaps you have not "lovingly" pointed out those areas where he needs to grow, and may not have been honest enough to listen to him when he tried to help you. If that is the case, you need to face your own need for growth, and then urge your husband to return to a process where growth will be on both of your parts.

He may not at first be willing. Have him reflect on this thought. He can easily divorce you, and even marry "the other woman". That may take a year or so. Then, it will take another year or so before the rose-colored glasses come off and true growth begins. At that point, he will realize that the second relationship is not that much different than the first. While he will then wonder what might have happened if he had tried to work things out with you, it will be too late. However, it is not too late now.

A three-month period of marriage counseling will tell him either that your relationship will not work, or that happiness has been under his nose all along. Either way, he has nothing to lose. Three months is long enough to see changed behavior as genuine, but not so long to condemn you to some sort of therapeutic limbo.

<u>KEY POINTS</u>

- <u>Power</u>: Another spouse cannot make you happy. Another look at yourself can.
- <u>Success</u>:
  - o Intimacy with one person can spark your growth, and bring you to new depths of maturity.
  - o A watered-down relationship with two persons has lost that intensity.

b. Who Are You Cheating On?

QUESTION: *My husband is cheating on me. He told me that life is too short, and that he shouldn't be "condemned" to one relationship. I am so angry. Why is he being such a jerk?*

ANSWER

We have just seen that many of those who have affairs picture that their marital vow denies them fun by restricting them to one person, rather than a creative vow freeing them from interference and for intimacy.

On the premise that a picture is worth a thousand words, if you are contemplating on having or are having an affair, humor me by engaging in a fantasy. While both men and women have affairs, let us picture you as a man.

I am going to put you up in a magnificent mansion for a year, complete with indoor and outdoor pools, the best of food and clothing, and acre upon acre of manicured lands. But, there is a hitch. You must agree not to leave the grounds. Not wanting you to be alone, you have a choice. You can either have one gorgeous woman to stay with you or ten. Which would you choose?

Given what is going on now, my guess is that you probably would giggle and devilishly pick ten women, imagining a sexual fantasy come true. But, there is a problem. As soon as any one woman would get too close, they would spot a flaw in your character, perhaps urging you to control your temper or be less selfish. Having nine other women at your beck and call, you could easily "dump" the first woman for any of the other nine. At the end of your year, you would emerge from the mansion claiming great sex, but having had very little true intimacy.

By contrast, if you chose one beautiful woman, she would eventually spot that same flaw, and you might well have a knock down, drag out argument, followed perhaps by a number of days filled with tension, the silent treatment, and you checking your meatloaf for cut glass. But eventually, not wanting to live alone for the rest of the year, and realizing that she had a valid point, you would begin to again talk. Not being able to run away from yourself, you would have emerged a happier, more fulfilled person than when you entered, claiming a little less sex, but a lot more intimacy.

Therefore, having an affair does not make any sense. Contrary to our culture, having more results in you having less. Adultery, often described as "cheating on your spouse" is really cheating on yourself. If you do not wake up to the truth within this story, then you will continue your affair, one day coming to the harsh realization that all this time you have been tragically running hard in the wrong direction after a ghost.

OUR MAP: *Relational Fallout*

PRINCIPLES and PROBLEMS
How our principles helped solve these problems.

<u>INSECURITY</u>: Adultery is a lack of belief in your spouse and a false belief that true happiness will come from a new person.

<u>POWER</u>: Jealousy is a lack of belief in yourself, fearing that your spouse will spot your flaws and leave you.

<u>SUCCESS</u>: Empowered by a belief in yourself, you are able to continually grow by deepening your relationship with others, not running after more people, but rather more depth with the same people.

FURTHER READING

- Snyder, Douglas K., Douglas H. Baucon and Kristina Coop Gordon, <u>Getting Past the Affair: A Program to Help You Cope, Heal, and Move On—Together or Apart</u>, New York, Guilford Press, 2007.
- Subotnik, Rena B., and Gloria G. Haras, <u>Surviving Infidelity: Making Decisions, Recovering from the Pain</u>, 3rd Ed., Avon, MA, Adams Media, 2005.

D. Addictions

Well, think of the weight of all those confused ideas and resulting emotions that we have discussed in the last chapter. They combine to become an albatross laid across the shoulders of a person, and no matter how broad those shoulders may be, a person looks for a way to cope, a solution simpler and quicker than, as some people think, endlessly exploring one's navel in therapy.

Hence, we see the psychological component of many addictions, which when added to predisposing factors such as genetics, powerfully lead someone so far and so deep down the wrong path as to require extensive help to emerge from having been so lost.

1. Alcoholism

a. Signs of Addiction

QUESTION: *While I know roughly what to look for in terms of how much a person drinks to determine if they are addicted, what are some of the psychological signs?*

ANSWER

Alcoholism is rampant in our society. To the alcoholic, the bottle offers a reward for a hard day's work, solace if the day has gone poorly, and the knowledge that relief will come immediately and without having to talk about their feelings.

Therefore, when their drinking becomes a problem either at home or work, or both, there will be huge resistance to give up such a wonderful ally. The mind will invent numerous ways to fend off the attempts of family and friends to help them. Here are but a few.

- **DENIAL**: Not admitting they have a problem.
- **PROJECTION**: Blaming others for their behavior.
- **RATIONALIZATION**: Making excuses to justify why they need to drink.
- **MINIMIZING**: Making light of how serious their problem is.
- **AVOIDING PEOPLE**: Socializing less so as to use drugs more without being noticed.
- **AVOIDING FEELINGS**: Intellectualizing feelings or using humor to avoid facing their poor self-esteem.
- **MANIPULATION**: Shrewdly influencing others by guilt to cover their behavior, often ensnaring family members to become co-dependent.
- **HOSTILITY**: Blowing up so as to blow away any attempt to confront them.

Confronting someone abusing alcohol means confronting the psychological defenses that I have just listed. Doing so is not being cruel, but actually is an act of kindness and love. Not doing so is becoming part of the problem, instead of the solution.

Some questions to ask to help someone face a drinking problem, for example, are:

- *Is a party not fun without a drink?*
- *Is your drinking affecting your family or work?*
- *Do you drink in the morning?*
- *Do you look forward to your next drink?*
- *If you only drink too much on weekends, do you think that it's not a problem?*
- *Have you tried unsuccessfully to cut down or quit?*

b. Treating Alcoholism

QUESTION: *A friend of our family has been lost in alcoholism for years, but now has thankfully agreed to get help. What exactly will treatment mean for him?*

ANSWER

If you are finally able to get someone who is addicted to alcohol into treatment, it will be multi-faceted. It begins with "*detoxification*", a process where he will be helped to withdraw from (eliminate) alcohol from his body. As this process can be life threatening (possible symptoms being a grand mal seizure, epileptic attack, tremors, high temperature, and high blood pressure), it generally calls for in-patient treatment so as to safely withdraw in a hospital setting.

Treatment will then graduate to *intensive outpatient care* often consisting of three days a week for a period of weeks. Usually, the in-patient facility also conducts the intensive outpatient care. Finally, a person improves to the stage when *weekly outpatient therapy* will suffice.

At first, the treatment will try to deal with the abuse itself, achieving abstinence and then trying to sustain it by looking at the consequences and patterns of using, as well as the triggers for using (people, places, things, situations, feelings, and thoughts that promote use).

Gradually, whatever pain alcohol has dulled will have to be faced, investigating any underlying psychological causes, such as low self-esteem and depression. Dealing with these is later in treatment due to not wanting to give a person another reason to drink.

Throughout this entire time, people are expected to participate in *Alcoholics Anonymous*, being asked to attend 90 meetings in 90 days. Why so much? Because the danger of relapse is so high, daily support in as many forms as possible is vital.

Also, as numerous studies have revealed, its causes are not just psychological, but also genetic, usually evidenced by numerous relatives suffering from the same problem. Hence, the goal is not controlled drinking, but abstinence and a new lifestyle, the high degree of change calling for a high degree of ongoing and multifaceted support.

Lastly, a resource that you may find very helpful is:
The National Clearinghouse for Alcohol and Drug Information (1-800-729-6686).

2. Drug Abuse

The intent of this book is not be a comprehensive exploration of addictions, but rather to show how addictions are one more example of looking for happiness in all the wrong places. We have been concentrating on adults who are addicted, so I would like to take time to share with you two letters about children that I received from parents, both letters touching concerns common to many.

a. The Whys of Teen Drug Abuse

QUESTION: *I am a father with a teenager who uses drugs. While I have explained how drugs will physically effect him, my son seems to have heard this over and over again in school. I'm not sure how to reach him. Do you have any ideas?*

ANSWER

While the ill effects of drug abuse are well documented, the reasons behind the abuse strangely receive less attention. In response to the question of this father, I suggested talking to his son to discover why he takes drugs. Discovering his motivation gets more to the core of the problem, let alone getting father and son closer. But, I did give five reasons that I have seen over time.

1. **PEER PRESSURE**: Many teens experiment with drugs rather than running the risk of seeming odd or abnormal. The desire for acceptance and their fear of rejection are powerful emotions. But, as "you can't please all the people all the time", parents should encourage autonomy and independent thinking. Teens may discover that the courage of their convictions may win them some true friends and challenge those who are so insecure that they must pressure others.

2. **REBELLION**: Instead of having learned to condescendingly please others, some adolescents express their desire for independence by breaking rules that they know will "drive my parents crazy". Yet, this is an example of cutting one's nose to spite one's face, the drug abuse hurting self more than others. Teens should be encouraged to express their anger, but to do so in ways that will help rather than hinder their own growth.

3. **IDENTIFICATION**: Still other teens use drugs not to rebel against parents, but to identify with them. If a parent brags about how much liquor they can hold, or makes a ritual of "tying one on" every Saturday night, the adolescent may see drug abuse as a rite of passage into adulthood. So, condemning smoking pot while sipping your fourth martini sends a dangerous double message.

4. **PLEASURE**: Some use marijuana to relax and be sociable, while others gravitate to stronger drugs such as cocaine, hoping to flee depression and find perfect happiness. Yet, the pursuit of happiness is an ongoing and challenging process rather than an attainable goal, and its relative achievement is won by facing life rather than escaping from it. And sadly, cocaine use gives a high followed by a deep low, making the person want to quickly get back to the high by taking more; hence, the addiction.

5. **MEANING**: Amazingly, some teens are again turning to hallucinogen drugs like LSD in a search for meaning, hoping their "trip" will bring them from a state of boredom or emptiness to an esoteric and even religious level of profound insight. What a sad commentary this is upon our often shallow and materialistic culture, and what a strong calling for organized religion to take a more proactive stance on leading us to a better sense of values and priorities.

b. Kids Exposed to Drugs

QUESTION: *My friend's son plays with someone whose father has a drug habit. My friend doesn't want her son exposed to a man using drugs, but has been told by the man's wife that there is no problem, as she does not use drugs herself. However, she will not confront or leave her husband. What should I tell my friend to do?*

ANSWER

In response to this second letter, I agreed with the mother in not allowing her son to be exposed to a man using drugs. Of course, I said that this meant dealing with conflict, which would be uncomfortable for everyone.

The mother would have to tell her son that he could no longer go to the home of his friend, being honest and sensitive as to why, and dealing with his angry and hurt feelings. She would have to have a prolonged discussion with her son about drug abuse, now from a much more personal than simply academic perspective.

The more difficult portion of the solution would be talking directly to either the father of her son's friend, or his mother, or both. She should not be sarcastic or mean, just direct, assertively explaining her values and the rationale for her decision.

This latter discussion will be very helpful to this other couple. It would seem that the mother of the other boy is enabling the drug problem of her husband, rather than telling him that he must squarely address the issue of drug abuse. For the mother writing me to be drawn into that spider web of enabling behaviors would not do anyone any good—the father continuing to use drugs, the mother continuing to feel helpless, and both boys continuing to be exposed to drug abuse.

While speaking up, I bet, produced an uncomfortable argument, this mother needed to see it as an act of love to the other family, rather than being rigid and difficult herself. She was the healthy parent, and was simply trying to offer health to this other family by drawing a very understandable line in the sand. Her action provided an opportunity for the other family to heal, namely, for the mother to be more assertive, the father to seek treatment, and the son to observe better coping skills.

I realized that this process would be a bumpy ride, to say the least. But, loving your neighbor does not mean ignoring their issues, especially when they impact on your own family. It means being brave enough to lovingly ask someone to change, but then enforcing the consequences of their own choice.

<u>KEY POINT</u>

- <u>Power</u>:
    - o Do what you think is best for you and your family instead of worrying about an argument with the neighbors or even resistance from your own son.
    - o Taking back your power to do what you think is right may help an enabling spouse of someone abusing drugs to do the same.

3. Eating Disorders

QUESTION: I have a good friend who suffers from bulimia. I don't know much about eating disorders. Could you help me understand them better?

ANSWER

Addictions are not restricted to alcohol or drugs, but can take other forms, such as eating disorders or gambling. First, let us take a look at the eating disorders, discussing their types, causes and treatment.

1. <u>**TYPES**</u>: There are two main eating disorders: bulimia and anorexia nervosa.

a. <u>***Bulimia***</u>: involves two or more episodes per week of "binge" eating, where a person consumes 5,000 to 20,000 calories in high fat foods such as ice cream, doughnuts, and candy. As the person feels out of control while binging, these episodes are typically followed by "purging" or self-induced vomiting to prevent weight gain. Also used are laxatives, diuretics, and strict fasting for the same purpose.

b. <u>***Anorexia Nervosa***</u>: involves such an intense fear of getting fat that the person allows their body weight to fall at least 15% below the norm, and feels fat even when emaciated. Women in the latter stages of this disorder often experience the absence of their menstrual cycle. Only 5-10% of anorexic patients are men.

2. <u>**CAUSES**</u>:

a. <u>***Societal Pressure***</u>: The pressure on women in our society to be thin is immense. It is bad enough trying to live up to a *Revlon* ad, the *Sports Illustrated* Swim Suit issue, or images splashed across the pages of *People* magazine, but there are even ads now that portray women looking like emaciated waifs as the ideal woman.

b. <u>***Family Dynamics***</u>:

(1). <u>*Bulimia*</u>: The person may come from a family typified by hostility and/or detachment, the absence of love resulting in a craving for the presence of food. Think of it, one of the first ways that love was communicated was a baby's bottle.

(2). <u>*Anorexia Nervosa*</u>: Here, families are typified by a lack of hostility, and a presence of over-nurturing and over-protectiveness. If the person doubts her own inner strength, the adolescent transition into adulthood can be scary, and force them to increase their attractiveness by decreasing their weight. Also, the overprotection is experienced as over controlling, and the one thing that can be controlled as a form of adolescent rebellion is what you put in your mouth.

3. **TREATMENT**: Whether you binge or purge, or whether you can never be thin enough, the end result is feeling depressed for "not measuring up". This is where therapy can begin to attack the underlying problem, helping a person to realize that they have set impossible standards of perfection both for their bodies and their souls. Gradually, they are helped to relax, see their value as coming from within instead of from without, and set their own goals for their body weight, career, and marriage.

Group therapy and support groups like Overeaters Anonymous help by assisting people to see that they are not alone, and by learning what has or has not worked for others. Finally, family and friends must try to examine their own prejudices and behavior, so that a healthier person is not placed back into an unhealthy environment.

4. Gambling

Shot by Slots

QUESTION: *I'm retired. Work was all I knew. With a lot of time on my hands, I went to Atlantic City with other seniors, and lost a bundle on the slot machines. The more I'd lose, the more I'd hope to win back. But now I've dug myself quite a hole. What can you tell me about gambling?*

ANSWER

I live in New Jersey. For a state hosting the Casinos of Atlantic City, you would think more would be written about gambling. By no means am I an expert, but I can pass along a few facts that might prove helpful if you or a friend suffer from an addiction to gambling.

1. <u>**WHO**</u>:
   - 80% of those who gamble know when to stop.
   - 15% spend more than they can afford, wake up embarrassed, and repentantly go home to their spouse and family with their proverbial tail between their legs.
   - 5% are compulsive gamblers, who continue on a downward spiral that sees fortunes and family erode.
   - The average debt in 2006 for those who called the hotline of the Council on Compulsive Gambling of New Jersey (1-800-Gambler) was $28,049, this coming from those whose average income was only $44,607.
   - People with time tend to be vulnerable, such as seniors who are retired, and sales persons and some professionals who can manage their own time.

2. <u>**CREEPING CRIME**</u>:
   - 90% of compulsive gamblers will gradually slip into crime to cover past debts or future dreams of the big score.
   - 20-30% of New Jersey inmates may be compulsive gamblers. At an approximate cost of $25,000 per inmate per year, addictive gambling is

a problem that hits all taxpayers in the pocket, let alone clogging court calendars.

3. **WHY**:

- *ACTION*: The reasons behind the addiction are not simply money, but more often the euphoric excitement that a potential win produces. Slot machines, especially video poker, have been referred to as the crack cocaine of gambling. New studies suggest that such risk taking increases dopamine levels in the brain, encouraging continued gambling even when losing.

- *ESCAPE*: In addition, some perceive the chance to escape a "humdrum" life or depressed mood, hoping to hit it big to avoid feeling small.

- *ATTENTION*: Some research points to parents who provided gifts and money as a guilty reparation for the lack of quality time they spend with their children. If money then equals love, or the power to get love, then gambling is seen as a possible quick fix.

4. **ENTICING ENVIRONMENT**: Casinos typically have no clocks or windows to remind you how long you have been gambling, no seats in which to relax unless you sit to bet, waitresses to get you a drink rather than have you get up and perhaps out, bright and colorful lighting to appeal to the senses, chips instead of "real money", machines that encourage you to bet more to win more, and the clinking of encouraging quarters falling noisily to announce that you are a winner.

5. **TREATMENT**:

   a. Certainly, the person must be helped to challenge the meaning of money, and seeing that one can be happy and a good provider without necessarily rolling in money like Scrooge McDuck.

   b. Apart from a shift in thinking, there needs to be a shift in behavior. As the person is suffering from an addiction, abstinence instead of "cutting back" is required. Therefore, the person needs support, and should seek treatment, as well as join Gamblers Anonymous.

   c. Family needs to be counseled as to how they can help, usually by removing access to money as much as possible. This includes handing over paychecks to a spouse, taking away all credit cards, and having bank accounts that require a counter signature. Families need help in seeing these actions as kind instead of cruel, and in resisting manipulations for sympathy, such as a loan from parents to replace money that has been lost, as often loaning money will mean losing money.

d. Finally, as the game is ending, depression and thoughts of suicide may be beginning, and counseling will return over and over again to the notion of self-esteem coming from internal qualities rather than external money. The love of family and friends, even when the money is gone, will be essential to recovery.

OUR MAP: *Addictions*

PRINCIPLES and PROBLEMS
How our principles helped solve these problems.

<u>POWER</u>: To please peers or punish parents is to hand over control of your growth to them.

<u>SUCCESS</u>: Reaching for instant gratification instead of gradual growth is burning yourself out by chasing a ghost.

<u>FURTHER READING</u>

- Costin, Carolyn, <u>The Eating Disorder Sourcebook</u>, 3rd Ed., New York, McGraw Hill, 2007.

- DiClemente, Carlo C., <u>Addiction and Change: How Addictions Develop and Addicted People Recover</u>, New York, Guilford Press, 2003.

- Gracier, Richard I., <u>A New Prescription for Addiction</u>, Tuggerah, NSW, Elite Books, 2007.

- Grinols, Earl L., <u>Gambling in America</u>, Cambridge, UK, Cambridge University Press, 2004.

- Herzog, David B., Debra L. Franko, and Pat Cable, <u>Unlocking the Mysteries of Eating Disorders</u>, New York, McGraw Hill, 2008.

- Johnson, Vernon E., <u>Intervention: How to Help Someone Who Doesn't Want Help</u>, Minneapolis, Johnson Institute, 1986.

- Ksir, Charles, Carl L. Hart, and Oakley Ray, <u>Drugs, Society and Human Behavior</u>, 12th Ed., New York, McGraw Hill, 2008.

- O'Farrell, Timothy J., and William Fals-Stewart, <u>Behavioral Couples Therapy for Alcoholism and Drug Abuse</u>, New York, Guilford Press, 2006.

CHAPTER FIVE

GETTING BACK ON TRACK

In the last chapter, we looked at ways in which we can get lost. Now, let us look at ways to help us stay on or get back on track.

Communication skills will seem a natural for me to mention, but you will probably be surprised by my inclusion of anger and divorce.

As you will see, anger gets a bad reputation, the problem not being *that* you get angry, but *how*. Unless you only befriend or marry your clone, you will encounter many differences, some healthy and some not. If you are to work through those differences, effective arguing is important instead of seething and fuming now only to explode later.

And, if your spouse refuses to work with you in creating a healthy marriage, then I doubt your happiness will be served by being stuck in an unhealthy one. While much has to happen before you decide on a divorce, getting one will be simply putting a name on the reality of a dead relationship, having asserted your right to be happy, and to have a spouse who either grows or goes.

A. Communication

1. How to Listen

QUESTION: My wife and I are always fighting. She says that I just don't listen. I don't know what she means. Are there some simple things that I could do that would help?

ANSWER:

Essential to learning to love others and find happiness is being able to communicate well. When I mention the word "communicate", your first thought is probably to talk. But as the goal is to be in communion with someone, then you also must learn to listen.

Let us take the humble course, and begin by explaining how best to listen to the other before speaking ourselves. While my examples primarily relate to married couples, most of these suggestions can be adapted to any two people who wish to get closer.

1. **PAY ATTENTION**: When you talk, sit close and face each other. Do not try to talk and watch TV, read the paper, prepare dinner, or play a game on the computer. Looking directly at one another will help you see important non-verbal communications like a frown, a raised eyebrow, or a tear in the eye. Missing that will mean missing the power of what is being said or not said.

2. **SLOW DOWN**: The goal is not to rush through a talk with your spouse so as to get back to a ball game, but rather to continually get to know one another. Who your spouse was when you married him or her, and who they are now could be quite different, as each of us continues to grow. Show your spouse how important he or she is by carving out some time for one another, at least one, uninterrupted hour every week. Did I say a whole hour? Yup!

3. **DON'T GET DEFENSIVE**: If you are constantly interrupting your spouse, then you are trying to prepare your answer before fully hearing what your spouse has to say. While you can do two things at once, you cannot do them well. Try to hear what your spouse needs from you, instead of only hearing a complaint about your behavior. Your spouse is asking because he or she believes in you. Your spouse wants your love, not a debate.

4. **<u>DO SHOW EMPATHY</u>**: Try to feel what your spouse feels. Put yourself in their shoes. This is different from sympathy, which is to feel sorry *for* someone; instead it is to feel *with* them. This is a strenuous, but silent activity, where you try to imagine how you would feel if you were your spouse. It is a bridge that you build between you and your spouse, showing them that you care enough to come over to their side and feel their pain, even if you disagree with everything that they have said.

5. **<u>PARAPHRASE</u>**: To show your spouse that you have done your homework, summarize what they have said, not just their ideas, but also their feelings. If you get it wrong, then you would summarize it again, until your spouse agrees that you have captured the heart of what was said. This is not, therefore, a word-for-word tape recording, but rather showing your spouse that you understand the gist of what they were saying.

As paraphrasing (sometimes described as *active listening* or *reflexive listening*) is probably the most important skill to possess, let me give you an example to make sure you understand how it works. Let's suppose that you and your wife have been arguing, and she, wanting to make amends, tells you that she is preparing a special dinner for you tomorrow night. She asks what time she can expect you, and you tell her that you can certainly be home by seven o'clock.

At eight o'clock the next evening, you walk in the door and find your wife very upset. She says, "Where have you been? Dinner is ruined! You could have at least called me to tell me that you were going to be late. I really wonder whether you love me."

As she has been talking, your mind has been building up your defense. You think to yourself, "What a bitch. Did it ever occur to her that I may have had an emergency at work? No, all she cares about is her damn dinner. But, I really don't want to be in the dog house, so what can I say to shut her up. Oh, I know. I'll invite her out for dinner." When she finishes what she has to say, you then say, "I'm sorry. How about I take you out for dinner?"

Even if she concedes to going out to dinner, a golden opportunity has been missed. What could you have said instead? Well, if you paraphrased, it might have sounded like this: "Are you saying that you think that I don't love you because I didn't call?" Now you are hitting the nail on the head. Now you are addressing the central issue, and so dinner or no dinner, she will know that you heard her, that you addressed her concern, and that you probably then do love her.

Having done all of the above, it is now finally your turn to respond. While what I just described may seem like pouring glue all over the process of talking to each other, it will help get your talks unstuck by zeroing in on the core issue instead of getting lost in surface issues. The result will be a smile and a hug, instead of yelling and a slammed door. What do you have to lose? Give it a try.

2. How to Talk

QUESTION: Last issue, you told one husband "how to listen" to his wife, ending with "It is now finally your turn to respond". I wonder if you could tell another curious husband your advice on "how to talk".

ANSWER

OK, I know that you are dying to finally speak, so here are some ideas that will make the other person better able to hear what you will say.

1. **EXPRESS (*DO NOT SUPPRESS*) YOUR FEELING**: Tell your spouse how you are feeling. Do not try to avoid telling them, or indefinitely postpone it. If you are angry, for instance, holding your feelings in today may well lead to an explosion tomorrow. As the emotional force of four past issues get squeezed into one present issue, you end up yelling and "looking like a jerk", your spouse ends up hurt, and the issue still is not resolved.

If you have ever had an argument that has gotten out of hand, later wondering how so small an issue could have produced so big a reaction, my guess is that you have been suppressing what you are feeling. The explosive argument was the eruption of those pent-up issues. So, instead of holding them in, let them out. The nervousness you feel about expressing them is actually your ally, helping you to be careful when you speak instead of being so angry that you cut someone off at the knees.

2. **FOCUS ON YOUR FEELINGS, NOT HER BEHAVIOR**: Focus on your feelings and not her behavior. If she did something that hurt you, tell her more about how it made you feel, and less about what she did wrong. If she hears your need and sees how to help, then she tends to be less defensive and listens more to what you are saying. But, if you list a litany of her sins, then she digs in her heels and prepares to knock down the case that you have been building up against her. Remember, your goal is intimacy, not victory.

3. **FOCUS MORE ON SUBSTANCE THAN STYLE**: I realize that you may be nervous about looking "dumb" when you open your heart, especially if you are like most men who have been trained to not express feelings, but your spouse is not looking for you to be William Shakespeare, just to be open and honest. If your spouse senses that you are struggling to reveal your inner soul, then, if

they really love you, they will listen patiently, respecting your courage to trust their love.

4. **<u>STICK WITH ONE ISSUE</u>**: Try not to respond to the constructive criticism of your spouse with, "Oh yeah, well you're no prize either!" You will have your hands full with one issue, so avoid playing tit-for-tat, which only moves you further and further away from the main point to a point where you feel lost in a forest of ping-pong accusations.

5. **<u>PROPOSE A SOLUTION</u>**: A big difference between nagging and being assertive is offering a solution. While your proposal may be altered or replaced, it will be clear to your spouse that you are trying to be positive, hoping to work together to create a better union instead of pushing her away by painstakingly pointing out the depressing cracks in your marriage.

6. **<u>BE ROMANTIC</u>**: *How* you talk may help *what* you are going to say. Sit next to your spouse and hold their hand. Talk in the living room with soft music and candlelight instead of the kitchen under lights so bright that you could perform surgery. Combine sensitivity with assertiveness, and again remember that your goal is not to win, but to become closer.

7. **<u>BE BRAVE</u>**: I know that talking openly means risking being criticized or rejected. But, it also means deepening your love. Realize that you are not stupid. You married your spouse for a reason. Give him or her the benefit of the doubt, and you the marriage that you always wanted.

OUR MAP: *Communication*

PRINCIPLES and PROBLEMS
How our principles helped solve these problems.

INSECURITY: To interface with the other you must openly face yourself.

POWER: To define self but in relationship with others.

SUCCESS: To become more of you, you need to listen with empathy, talk with truth and relate with caring to the other.

FURTHER READING

- Bolton. Robert, People Skills: How to Assert Yourself, Listen to Others, and Resolve Conflicts, New York, Simon & Schuster, 1979.
- Cahn, Dudley D., Conflict in Intimate Relationships, New York, Guilford Press, 1992.
- McKay, Matthew, Martha Davis, and Patrick Fanning, Messages: The Communication Skills Book, Oakland, CA, New Harbinger Publications, 1995.

B. Anger

How to Get Angry

QUESTION: My wife says that I have a problem with my temper, that I blow up all the time, and that she's scared of me. But aren't you supposed to get your anger out?

QUESTION: People say that I'm moody. While I do get a little sarcastic at time, I try hard to hold my anger in. If that's wrong, what's right?

ANSWER

It is all right to get angry, for if we are different, we must argue to resolve those differences. The trick is to argue productively. Anger can be expressed in three ways:

- Aggressively,
- Passive-aggressively, or
- Assertively.

AGGRESSIVE ANGER: is overkill. When you yell, throw an ashtray, punch a hole in the wall, or threaten to punch someone, people become frightened, focusing more on how you are talking than on what you are saying. They may also wrongly assume that you are incapable of being gentle and caring, and so your friends do not invite you back and your spouse asks for a divorce. Too much anger leads to too little love.

PASSIVE-AGGRESSIVE ANGER: is what I call "sneaky anger". Being scared to "bite the hand that feeds you", you express your anger in an indirect and covert manner. Your sarcasm stings, your silent treatment chills the house, and your procrastination frustrates everyone to death. But, while everyone knows that you are mad, no one knows why, and most people just give you a wide berth rather than baby you with twenty questions to discover what is wrong.

ASSERTIVE ANGER: is the mean between the extremes. It is calm and rational rather than violent and aggressive, and direct and open rather than indirect and secretive. A few helpful hints are:

1. *Use "I" instead of "You" Statements* so as to avoid blaming or putting down the other. "Honey, I'm feeling left out; I wish you'd talk with me" is less threatening than "You never talk to me; you just sit there and pout".

2. Stick with the **Present in Specific Terms instead of the Past in Vague Generalizations**, pinpointing the problem rather than hurling accusations at one another. "I was hurt last night when you yelled at me" pinpoints the problem, whereas "You always yell at people; last night at me, last week at Billy" only promotes defensiveness.

3. *Combine the "I" Statement with a Solution*, as anger without a proposed remedy is called "nagging". Your solution should, however, be a suggestion, not an order, for the purpose of your talk is to discuss rather than dictate the outcome, producing intimacy, not a winner.

OUR MAP: *Anger*

PRINCIPLES and PROBLEMS
How our principles helped solve these problems.

<u>POWER</u>: Do be assertive and state your mind.

<u>INSECURITY</u>: Do not let your fear produce silence, sarcasm or aggression.

FUTHER READING

- Bower, Sharon Anthony, and Gordon H. Bower, <u>Asserting Yourself: A Practical Guide for Positive Change</u>, Cambridge, MA, Da Capo Press, 1991.

- Lerner, Harriet, <u>The Dance of Anger</u>, New York, Harper & Row, 1985.

- McKay, Matthew, Peter D. Rogers, and Judith McKay, <u>When Anger Hurts: Quieting the Storm Within</u>, 2nd Ed., Oakland, CA, New Harbinger Publications, 2003.

- Middleton-Moz, Jane, Lisa Tener, Peaco Todd, <u>The Ultimate Guide to Transforming Anger: Dynamic Tools for Healthy Relationships</u>, Deerfield Beach, FL, Health Communications, 2004.

- Nay, W. Robert, <u>Taking Charge of Anger: How to Resolve Conflict, Sustain Relationships and Express Yourself Without Losing Control</u>, New York, The Guilford Press, 2004.

C. Forgiveness

The Three Elements of Forgiveness

QUESTION: I don't understand forgiveness. It seems so weak, as if you're letting someone get away with murder and opening the door for them to abuse you all over again. Am I right?

ANSWER

No, but it is a hard concept to understand. There are really three elements defining forgiveness. Let's look at them.

1. <u>REPENTANCE</u>: A person must be genuinely contrite, truly sorry for having hurt you.

2. <u>CHANGE</u>: How do you know if someone is really sorry? By their behavior. This means reparation, not hurriedly reciting 5 Hail Mary's and 5 Our Fathers, but real change. Often, this simply means doing the opposite of what was done wrong. If sarcastic, then being kind as well as direct. If defaming the name of someone, then restoring their good name. If lying, then telling the truth. If stealing, then the restitution of monies.

    The goal here is not to hurt the person, but rather to save him. The hope is to start the person on a path towards renewal, realizing that he is in the process of creating who he is. The judgment of God is to accept our judgment, to allow us to have the consequences of our own actions. The punishment for being selfish is to **be** selfish. It is written on our soul, and no amount of fast talking will change that reality. A person is stuck with his or her choice for all eternity, and that is far more powerful than any pound of flesh that we extract from those who hurt us.

3. <u>PARDON</u>: Now comes what we understand as "forgiveness". It does not mean magically erasing a sin from someone's soul, but rather giving them another chance. Why? Because forgiveness is based less on the fact that the "forgiver" is a nice person, and more on the fact that the "forgivee" has the potential for change. We need to separate out person from behavior. For instance, if your son does something wrong, you should not say, "You are a

bad boy", but rather "You are a good boy who did something bad". Change is always possible, this, for instance, being one of the reasons why the religious community is against the death penalty.

But, what if after all this the person continues to hurt you? Then, you withdraw your forgiveness and separate yourself from the person so as to avoid being hurt. We tend to forget that in Christian theology, Jesus told his disciples "Whose sins you shall forgive, they are forgiven them. Whose sins you shall *retain*, they are *retained*." (John 20: 21-23).

To make this clearer, if I kept punching you in the nose and asking for your forgiveness, eventually, you would determine that enough is enough, tell me to leave, and even put up your fists to protect yourself. Are you being UnChristian? No, just UnStupid! God does not want you to be a punching bag, just to give others who are genuinely sorry a chance to change.

OUR MAP: *Forgiveness*

PRINCIPLES and PROBLEMS
How our principles helped solve these problems.

POWER: Forgiving is based more upon the inner potential of the offender to change than the outer kindness of the offended who forgives.

SUCCESS: The punishment for being selfish is to **be** selfish, grabbing for too much without concern for others robbing one of closeness with others.

FURTHER READING

- Casarjian, Robin, <u>Forgiveness: A Bold Choice for a Peaceful Heart</u>, New York, Bantam Books, 1992.
- Luskin, Fred, <u>Forgive for Love</u>, New York, Harper One, 2007.
- Simon, Sidney and Suzanne Simon, <u>Forgiveness: How to Make Peace with Your Past and Get on With Your Life</u>, New York, Time Warner Book Group, 1990.
- Smedes, Lewis B., <u>Forgive & Forget: Healing the Hurt We Don't Deserve</u>, San Francisco, Harper Collins, 1984.
- Spring, Janis Abrahms, <u>How Can I Forgive You?</u>, New York, Harper Collins, 2004.

D. Divorce

1. Coping with Divorce

QUESTION: My husband divorced me 3 months ago, saying that I was boring and had held him back from career advancements. I'm 42 and overweight. I haven't worked in years. Who'd want a middle-age, fat, unemployed woman with 2 kids?

ANSWER

I find the self-doubt expressed by this woman to be common. Reeling under the unfair criticism flowing from her husband, she had fallen into the trap of putting all the blame for the divorce on herself. She was torturing herself with bargaining, probably claiming that if she had lost a few more pounds or attended a few more business parties, then she could have saved her marriage.

The truth is, however, that just as it took two to make a marriage, it also takes two to break it. Her husband, hoping to enlist allies in this war to prove his innocence, projected blame to her and relished in the fact that she accepted it.

So, she and others like her should stop blaming themselves, and instead start evaluating their half of what went wrong.

- If she was overly dependent, then she should take stock of her considerable inner strengths.

- If she was shy and avoided social gatherings, she should force herself to slowly widen her circle of friends and acquaintances, not primarily to counterbalance her husband's negativity with positive comments, but rather to discover how much she has to offer.

- She should look for a job and not be discouraged if it takes time.

- When friendships form and compliments on job performance occur, her real, but hidden, self will finally come into focus.

Then, if **she** chooses, she will be ready to remarry, not feeling "lucky" to have found anybody, but taking her time to find someone who will love her as much as she loves them. As we know from our guiding principles, she should not give anyone the power to define her worth, not even her husband, no matter whether he is kind or cruel.

KEY POINTS

- <u>Insecurity</u>: No one is perfect. Do not put yourself down for being over-weight and unemployed. Not only can you can change those things, but you are also far more than those things.

- <u>Power</u>: Do not give the power to define your worth to any spouse, especially an angry one who is ducking blame by projecting it to you.

- <u>Success</u>: Having taken back your power, determine how you would like to grow and whom you might choose to marry, when and if you are ready.

2. Children and Divorce

QUESTION: A talk show said that kids aren't really all that affected by a divorce. Can that be true?

ANSWER

Nothing could be further from the truth. While a divorce may be necessary and best for the parents, the effects of divorce on children are many. Here are some of the main ones so that you can understand how to help your children cope with the divorce.

1. **MY FAULT?** Children worry that if they had been behaved better, the divorce may not have happened. Children need not only to be told that the divorce was not their fault, but also to be given a brief explanation of what is occurring so they can deal with it.

2. **SECURITY**: Young children, worried that their world is falling apart, that they may lose their room or have to move, need to be reassured that they will always be cared for and protected.

3. **IDENTITY**: Older children worry, "If I'm like dad, and mom no longer loves dad, maybe someday mom will no longer love me." Both parents have to reassure children that they will always be loved, and each parent has to honestly help the child identify those good and bad traits that parent has passed on, keeping one and gradually reforming the other.

4. **FEAR OF REJECTION**: Adolescents and young adults may so fear being rejected as to hide their deeper feelings, avoid arguments by giving in to keep peace, and live together before marrying, hoping to be safe by "testing the waters". However, lacking honest communication and true commitment dooms the relationship and produces a self-fulfilling prophecy. Again, allowing a child to talk through their understanding and feelings about the divorce will help them in being less worried about a sudden and unforeseen rejection, in being able to bravely face problems by being assertive when angry, and to plan for rather than fear an eventual marriage of their own.

5. **PARENTING THE PARENT**: As adults struggle with their feelings, they often turn to children for comfort and companionship, or for built-in maids or baby

sitters, and a boy or girl's childhood gets cut short. Parents should face their own insecurity in dating again, looking for companionship with other adults, not their children. And, while a child inheriting more chores in the absence of one parent may be a reality, that needs to be balanced with the reality that the decisions of two adults to divorce should not rob children of the joys of their youth.

6. **TAKING SIDES**: In bitter divorces, children are occasionally made to take sides, being pummeled with a litany of the faults of the other parent, being made to feel guilty if they enjoy a visit with the non-custodial parent (*let alone the new stepparent!*), or being enticed to move in with that parent by dangling their own room or more toys as the carrot on a stick. Being caught in the middle, they are forced to choose between disliking one parent or lying to the parent who pressures. Parents need to mourn the loss of their marriage rather than use their children as pawns in a chess game of blame.

7. **DISPLACING ANGER**: Parents, frustrated in their inability to vent anger on their absent spouse, may displace it onto their present children, who are trapped with nowhere to hide. Children themselves, not wanting to hurt their parents, may in turn displace anger onto parental surrogates like teachers, or perhaps onto their friends. Parents need to process their own anger with a friend or counselor, and help their children express rather than suppress their anger, showing the child that the parent is strong enough to handle it.

A final comment is that the above problems do not imply that parents should never divorce, just that the tragedy of divorce profoundly touches the lives of children, and that parents, while no longer husband and wife, need to continue to unselfishly work together as father and mother.

3. Dating After Divorce

QUESTION: I'm a middle-aged guy who has been divorced for about 6 months, and want to start dating. But, I'm scared of getting burned again. Got any suggestions?

ANSWER:

Eventually, after having healed from the divorce, especially in learning to love self in the midst of the rejection of the other, a person then may choose to gradually date so as to hopefully remarry. As the man who wrote this question decided he was ready, here are some things that I told him to consider.

1. **IS SHE DIVORCED?** It is unwise to date someone who is separated, but not divorced. Why? Because she may go back with her husband, leaving the tread marks of unsuccessful dating all over your heart. She may still have unresolved feelings for her husband, whether those be love, anger or sadness. Until those are resolved, you are taking a considerable risk in dating her, not only because you may be hurt, but your children will also get hurt if they get too close to her.

2. **CAN SHE LISTEN?** Communication is all too often viewed as a battle to determine who is right and who is wrong. Couples interrupt to make a point, get defensive when constructive criticism is offered, and try to win an argument instead of gain intimacy. Therefore, a key question is whether your date can really listen? Does she not only pay attention to what you are saying, but also seem to understand how you feel? Does she demonstrate empathy and understanding? If not, then growth will be a one-way street going in the opposite direction from you—all give and no get.

3. **CAN SHE TALK?** She should not only be able and willing to listen to your thoughts and feelings, but also reveal her own. Someone who wants to only take care of you, but not show their own clay feet, is probably hiding behind a mask of being a motherly caregiver. But, you want a wife, not a mother, which requires an equal relationship where each person is open to growth. After all, being married to Superwoman is boring. She never needs anything.

4. **HOW DOES SHE ARGUE?** When the first big argument erupts, do not get discouraged, or throw in the towel on the relationship. If she expresses anger by

yelling, being sarcastic, or giving you the silent treatment, then honestly tell her how her behavior affects you. If she apologizes, and then changes her behavior, you are dating a mature woman open to growth. However, if she either apologizes but then does not change, or does not apologize at all, telling you that this is the way she is and that you should "take me or leave me", leave her.

5. **LOOKING FOR CINDERELLA?** If you are squeamish after your divorce, and so continue to look for the perfect person, then you will die a perpetual bachelor. No matter who you find, she will be human, loaded with foibles and imperfections. The only thing that matters is whether she is open to growth through interaction with you. So, stop thinking of dating as going to the "Interpersonal Aisle" at Shop-Rite, and look for someone who is mature enough to take off her mask and be herself.

6. **LOOK IN THE MIRROR?** Please realize that all of the above also applies to you! The purpose for getting married is not to avoid loneliness, but rather to spark the growth of one another through an intense, exclusive, creative, and loving relationship. So, while looking at the speck in her eye, don't forget the plank in your own.

OUR MAP: *Divorce*

PRINCIPLES and PROBLEMS
How our principles helped solve these problems.

<u>INSECURITY</u>: Do not punish yourself for any mistakes made, just learn from them and do not make them twice.

<u>POWER</u>: A failing marriage does not make you a failure. Do not catch the projected blame that an angry spouse may be throwing at you.

<u>SUCCESS</u>: Grow through your divorce rather than around it, becoming more of who you want to be by facing your pain.

FURTHER READING

- Ahrons, Constance, <u>The Good Divorce: Keeping Your Family Together When Your Marriage Comes Apart</u>, New York, Harper Collins Publishers, 1994.
- Clapp, Genevieve, <u>Divorce & New Beginnings</u>, 2nd Ed., New York, John Wiley & Sons, 2000.
- Ellison, Sheila, <u>The Courage to be a Single Mother: Becoming Whole Again After Divorce</u>, San Francisco, Harper, 2000.

E. Humility

QUESTION: Why should I be humble? Being meek and mild only lets others cruise by you on the way to the top. Why does religion push being weak as a virtue?

ANSWER

A virtue that will help you in your search for happiness is humility. What is humility? It is neither eating humble pie, nor being so passive as to let other people walk all over you, but rather seeing yourself in relation to God. Think of the differences that makes us want to bow our heads and bend our knees. Here are but four.

- **Eternal**: We have a definite beginning and end. No matter how much you exercise, eat lean meat and vegetables, or take vitamins, 100 years from now, you will be dead. God is not limited by time, it being an understatement to call him the God of our Forefathers.

- **Omnipresent**: No matter how big your house is, you can only be in one room at a time. No matter how rich you become, you can only travel to one place at a time. God is everywhere.

- **Omniscient**: No matter how many degrees that you attain, no matter how brilliant you are, you never will know it all. God does.

- **Omnipotent**: Think of all who held and revered power: Ramses II, Julius Caesar, Napoleon, etc. They are all dead. In a former age when some philosophers aspired to be supermen, I remember a story of graffiti having been scribbled on a wall in Berlin. It said, "God is Dead—signed Nietzsche". The next day, written underneath was, "Nietzsche is Dead—signed God". Touché.

Get the point? Even if you achieve more than any human who ever lived, you are still dwarfed by God. Why do we act so proud? Why are we consumed with trying to get others to think that we are great? Why have we still not learned the lesson of Adam and Eve in the Garden of Eden?

Having humility will help you live by the principles that we espoused at the beginning of the book. As this is rather important, let me give more than the normal succinct summary at the end of this article. Consider two problems.

PROBLEM #1: Like Adam and Eve, we want what we cannot have. We rail against our limits, always wanting more, the latest and greatest never satisfying for long. Not seeing the big picture, we are condemned to jealously vie for position in the little picture.

SOLUTION: Arrogantly wanting it all and wanting it now is believing happiness to be a quantifiable product that you can buy and own, controlling your growth without having to personally stretch. But, happiness is a process of becoming qualitatively more and more loving, realizing that success is more than attaining material goods that do not last, but also and more importantly attaining a spiritual depth and maturity that transcends this life to the next.

OUR MAP: Humility—Problem #1

PRINCIPLES and PROBLEMS
How our principles helped solve these problems.

HAPPINESS: Not a onetime product that you buy and control, but a lifetime process of becoming more of who you were meant to be. Being humble enables you to see that God would not offer so small a gift to one created in His image.

SUCCESS: Be less greedy and more humble, ironically achieving greater happiness by reaching for fewer possessions.

PROBLEM #2: Fearing criticism and yearning for praise, we wear masks of superiority, hoping to fool others and even ourselves. But, as mentioned earlier in this book, unlike the masks of Halloween that so easily come off at evening's end, these personality masks become harder and harder to take off as each year passes, as we begin to believe the web of lies that we have so assiduously been spinning. Tragically, life becomes an exercise in futility, the frustrating pursuit of power being always and elusively just beyond our grasp.

SOLUTION: Instead, we need to relax and realize that no one is superior, that we are all insecure. Humility enables us to not seek to be perfect, but to grow in becoming more perfect. And, we need to define our worth by looking at our inner qualities, not our outer possessions or the opinions of others. We need to have the courage to take back the power that we have given others, face our weaknesses, and grow to be more and more like God, who by His very definition is Love.

OUR MAP: Humility—Problem #2

PRINCIPLES and PROBLEMS
How our principles helped solve these problems.

INSECURITY: Humility enables you to see your limits as normal, and to relax in your lifetime process of growth.

POWER: Being humble, you realize that masks are futile and funny, hiding a creation of God that is more beautiful than any mask, no matter how bejeweled it may be.

A closing thought is to ask you why Moses could deal with no longer being a Prince of Egypt, or Jesus with being born in a manger, growing up in an obscure village, and dying on a cross? Because they knew what really matters. So, if you want to "get ahead", then don't be penny-wise and pound-foolish. Don't choose a big house and car, but settle for a small soul. Learn what the Pharaohs of Egypt never did. Your gold chariot will not be coming with you to the next life, but your soul will. Spend more time working on what lasts, not simply on what glitters today but is tarnished tomorrow.

F. Prayer

Feeding Your Soul

QUESTION: Sometimes I feel like I'm running on empty. It's such a fight to survive in this world of competition and criticism. How can I recharge my batteries?

ANSWER

As we have seen, the journey to happiness involves a lifetime of travel filled with challenges, some of which will spark your growth, and some of which will derail it. During your journey, you need help.

My guide is a help, but you also need people who can understand and support your quest. In our competitive, materialistic culture, many will not only fail to understand your direction, but they will also work hard to persuade you to take a different path. Hence, you will need the loving support of your parents, your spouse, and your friends.

But, there is one support readily available but rarely used, God. He created you, wants you to be happy, and is available to talk with you every minute of every day. However, as we cannot see God, and cannot really see our souls, we often give both only lip service. Think about it, we eat three meals a day, taking good care of our bodies. Seldom, however, are we as generous when it comes to feeding our souls. If you are going to search for happiness, and believe in our principles that under gird your search, then you will ultimately encounter God, who can help you achieve an even greater degree of happiness. So, why not ask him for help? Why not talk to him?

Prayer is nothing other than talking with God. We think of prayer as reciting words from a book in a church or synagogue, but these prepared prayers are simply to help guide your conversation with God. You do not have to be limited to praying so formally. Anytime that you reflect on life and talk to your best friend (God) while doing it, even if you are angry with him, you are praying.

I once had a woman come to see me bereft after the death of her husband. Like so many who have lost their spouses, she could not understand why God had done that to her. Walking from room to room in her home, she screamed in anger at God. Being religious, she then became guilty about having been so disrespectful. I comforted her by telling her that she was simply praying, talking to God. With a friend, your conversations are not limited to soft and calm words, but can also involve the full range of emotions including anger, fear and laughter. Why would it be any different with God?

Therefore, in your journey, realize that you have a constant and loving companion, who created you, wants you to be happy, and will give you all the support you need. You just have to ask, and then, instead of always telling God what you want, listen to what He may say is in your best interest.

Open your mind to receive information from all sources. If you doubt the existence of God, do not lazily rest upon your doubts as an excuse, but rather work to resolve them. Why? Because otherwise your search will be limited and so too will be your resulting happiness. Moses wanted to commune with God atop Mount Sinai and was visibly transformed. Jesus wanted us to be perfect as our heavenly father is perfect. So, why not? Go for it all. You deserve it.

OUR MAP: Prayer

PRINCIPLES and PROBLEMS
How our principles helped solve these problems.

INSECURITY: The nice thing about God is that you need not even try hiding your insecurities. He sees them all.

POWER: Not giving others the power to define your worth does not mean not talking to others, especially to God who gives you free will and does not interfere with your choices.

SUCCESS: Your inner success is so important that I hope you use all the resources at your disposal, including talking with God.

CONCLUSION

Well, here we are at the end of my guide for your journey to happiness. You may well have disagreed with me on a few points here or there, but I hope that you know that my only desire was to offer you suggestions and short cuts that it has taken me a lifetime to discover. As this book has clearly stated, you are the captain of your own ship, holding the power to decide in which direction you will travel.

Hence, use these ideas in any way that you choose. But, please do not fall into the trap of thinking that you are getting too old to change. If you are still breathing, you can still grow. While your personality is largely formed by the time you are eighteen, adulthood should be the time for us to gradually increase our strengths and decrease our weaknesses. If you are shy, you need to be more social. If dependent, more independent. If too competitive, more cooperative. And if you are a workaholic, to judge yourself less by what you do and more by who you are.

I often see more growth from the elderly than from those far younger, older people knowing not to waste what valuable time remains in their lives. To think that we would pass some magic age where growth would no longer be possible would be an insult to the creativity of both our Creator and ourselves. So, no matter how old you are, you can still change. The more that you change, the happier you can become, for happiness is not an end state; it is a process. Therefore, never waiver from your lifetime quest of creating an ever growing, ever expanding, ever more happy work of art: YOU.

INDEX

978-0-595-48057-9
0-595-48057-8

3378024